PROPHECY AND PROPHETS
THE DIVERSITY OF CONTEMPORARY
ISSUES IN SCHOLARSHIP

THE SOCIETY OF BIBLICAL LITERATURE
SEMEIA STUDIES

Vincent L. Wimbush, Editor

PROPHECY AND PROPHETS
THE DIVERSITY OF CONTEMPORARY ISSUES IN SCHOLARSHIP

edited by

Yehoshua Gitay

Society of Biblical Literature
Semeia Studies

Scholars Press
Atlanta, Georgia

PROPHECY AND PROPHETS
THE DIVERSITY OF CONTEMPORARY ISSUES IN SCHOLARSHIP

Library of Congress Cataloging in Publication Data

Prophecy and prophets : the diversity of contemporary issues in
  scholarship / edited by Yehoshua Gitay.
      p.   cm. — (The Society of Biblical Literature Semeia studies)
      Includes bibliographical references and indexes.
      ISBN 0-7885-0316-2 (pbk. : alk. paper)
      1. Prophets. 2. Prophecy—Comparative studies. 3. Middle East—
  Religion. 4. Bible. O.T.—Criticism, interpretation, etc.
  I. Gitay, Yehoshua. II. Series: Semeia studies.
  BS1198.P74 1996
  220.1'5—dc20   96-41270
                                                  CIP

Printed in the United States of America
on acid-free paper

TABLE OF CONTENTS

CONTRIBUTORS

Ronald E. Clements
Professor Emeritus, Kings College, University of London
8 Brookfield Road
Coton, Cambridge, CB3 7PT
England

James L. Crenshaw
Robert L. Flowers Professor of Old Testament
The Divinity School
Duke University
Durham, North Carolina 27708
USA

David Noel Freedman
Department of History
University of California at San Diego
9500 Gilman Drive 0104
La Jolla, California 92093
USA

Yehoshua Gitay
Isidore and Theresa Cohen Chair of Hebrew Language and
Literature
University of Cape Town
Rondebosch 7700
South Africa

Zefira Gitay
Department of Art History
University of Cape Town
Rondebosch 7700
South Africa

John R. Huddlestun
  Department of Philosophy and Religious Studies
  College of Charleston
  Charleston, South Carolina 29424
  USA

Herbert B. Huffmon
  Drew University
  SH-14
  Madison, New Jersey 07940
  USA

David L. Petersen
  Iliff School of Theology
  2201 South University
  Denver, Colorado 80210
  USA

Rolf Rendtorff
  Professor Emeritus, University of Heidelberg
  Buchenweg 21
  D-61184 Karben 1
  Germany

INTRODUCTION

Generations of readers have been inspired by the prophets and the literature ascribed to them. The scholarly world is not excluded. The history of scholarship on prophecy indicates that a number of fundamental questions revolving around the nature of the prophetic movement and the design of its literature are still unresolved. However, the presentation of fresh data, on the one hand, and the introduction of new scholarly focal interests, on the other hand, may stimulate new inquiries. For instance, new information regarding the genesis of prophecy may shed light on the history of the prophetic phenomenon, and the impact of recent literary methods is instrumental in reshaping the center of prophetic research from the autonomic oracle to the book as a whole. Prophetic scholarship is also influenced by the over all tendency in the study of the Humanities to apply interdisciplinary research, proposing as a result new insights into classical problems of prophetic studies, such as the presentation of the prophetic persona and the transfer from the prophetic charisma to the book.

Research on prophecy revolves around the following topics: the prophetic reality and its historical roots; the prophetic figure; the nature of prophetic literature; the political function of prophetic activity; the role of the institution in the composition of the prophetic book, the book itself in its editorial shape; and the perception of the later readers of the prophetic book. The study of prophetic phenomena from various angles, each of which also requires its own scholarly discipline, is the objective of the present volume.

The variety of approaches and the diversity of scholarly interests in prophecy, naturally invite the collaboration of eminent scholars, each of whom is able to represent a particular scholarly area of research and approach. Taken as a whole, the approaches and interests of the collaboration that is the present volume reflect the tensions and controversies that are part of research in prophecy.

The genesis of the prophetic tradition is the subject that opens the volume. The discoveries of literary archives at Mari, the city located on the middle Euphrates, reveal prophetic texts from the early second millennium. This material may shed fresh light on the pre-history of the biblical prophetic tradition. Scholars who seek to place the prophetic movement in the context of the ancient Near East search in the Mari archives for comparative philological evidence. Herbert B. Huffmon's essay, "The Expansion of Prophecy in the Mari Archives," traces the pre-biblical history of prophecy. A number of documents published recently enables Huffmon to unveil the pre-history of the prophetic tradition. On the basis of the Mari archives, Huffmon raises some fundamental questions, for example, regarding the identity of prophets in Mari. Were they ecstatics, announcers or public speakers? And what do we know about the obscure biblical term *nabi*? These are some of the questions to which he seeks answers in the study of the pre-biblical prophetic tradition.

The next essay has to do with the literature of biblical prophecy. How does one characterize the various prophetic functions in accordance with the biblical literature? In "Rethinking the Nature of Prophetic Literature," David L. Petersen analyses biblical literature in accordance with the characteristic features of the prophetic activity. This study uses a variety of approaches, seeking to answer the question: "what is prophetic literature"? This leads to the issue of the stylistic medium of this literature as a means of determining the various prophetic functions.

The prophets as individuals to various degrees and in different ways come into focus in the prophetic books. So discussion about the nature of the prophetic literature opens the door for the study of the portrayal of prophetic figures. The prophetic books are named after prophets, who are presented as taking an active role both through their speeches and through their patterns of behavior in the act of announcing God's message. What is the role of the prophetic persona in the presentation of the prophetic material? This is the issue discussed by Yehoshua Gitay in his article: "The Projection of the Prophet: A Rhetorical Presentation of the Prophet Jeremiah."

Attention is turned next to the prophetic office and the religious nature of the prophetic teaching. These issues are the subject-matter of David Noel Freedman's essay: "Between God and Man: Prophets in Ancient Israel." The essay focuses on the major features of the prophetic office: the prophet's experience of God; the call and the commission; the question of prophetic success or failure; the ethics of the prophetic religion; and the prophet as intercessor.

Discussions about the prophetic persona and the nature of the prophetic office provide a transition of sorts from focus upon the prophet himself to the book assigned to him. What made some prophets so successful that not only their names but also their speeches have been preserved, collected, and regarded as sacred books? What are the social functions of the prophetic books named after central prophetic figures? Ronald E. Clements' essay, "Max Weber, Charisma, and Biblical Prophecy," seeks to re-evaluate the relationship between the prophet and the book named after him. Drawing upon Weber's theory of charisma, Clements argues that the books that carry specific prophetic names were inspired by charismatic prophetic figures. He also argues that research should focus on the process of 'routinization,' that is, the process of establishing the prophetic speeches in written format (with some additions). Does the process of compiling the prophetic books function merely as a memorization? Or does it also function as a political response to the collapse of the institutions of the Judean and the Israelite societies during the eight and the sixth centuries, respectively? Clement's essay addresses these as well as other provocative issues.

The discussion regarding the cause and function of compiling the prophetic books motivates the study of the produced book in its given form. Rolf Rendtorff's essay, "The Book of Isaiah: A Complex Unity: Synchronic and Diachronic Reading," presents a programmatic demonstration of the editorial process of the book of Isaiah. The focus on the canonical shape of the prophetic books and their editorial design sheds light on the theological message proclaimed by the final form through systematic editorial activity. The author emphasizes the importance of the editorial and canonical process for understanding the message of the prophetic book as a whole.

A further problem relating to the canonical study of the prophetic books is whether the various passages, which constitute the book as a whole, are designed as a book in itself. For instance, are passages that might be considered as sporadic editorial products, such as the epilogue of the book of Joel, literary and theologically integrated in the prophetic book? In other words, is there a prophetic book in the full sense of a book, with prologue, body, and epilogue? This is the subject of James L. Crenshaw's essay, "Freeing the Imagination: The Conclusion to the Book of Joel."

Finally, the question of the readers' perception (not the authors') of the prophetic message is explored. An answer to this question is given by the artists who perpetuated the prophetic message through their work. How has this been captured by artists? Did they portray the prophetic message through the depiction of a prophetic scene or through the depiction of the prophetic persona? Zefira Gitay explores the poetics of the artistic presentation of prophecy in her study entitled: "Prophet and Prophecy: An Artistic Dilemma."

In conclusion, for our modern pluralistic period, the study of prophetic literature is a research of altered kinds. Pluralism rather than singularity is the key for constructive and unprejudiced research. The present volume seeks to mirror the diversity rather than minimizing its existence through the works of one kind of prophetic research.

Given the varieties of subjects in prophetic research and the different approaches that characterize current scholarship, it is important to preserve the various voices of research. How differently will we hear the rich symphony of current prophetic research? We must acknowledge that the different approaches derive from the employment of various methods of research, each of which is based on its own merit, leading to different directions in research. Only a combination of various essays, gathering together various schools, pursuing each approach and focus of interest, may constitute a satisfactory picture of prophetic research as a whole.

Currently, we witness a shift in prophetic paradigms of research. The synchronic approach is achieving legitimization. Many volumes and essays are composed in order to place the synchronic approach on the map of prophetic research. The present volume differs, however, in its scholarly aim; it does not seek to promote a sole direction in prophetic research. The present volume asks for the variety as a genuine reflection of scholarship. The presentation of the various essays constituting this volume assures a deeper understanding of the diverse issues in current prophetic research through the analysis of texts and the engagement of the attendant scholarly interpretive problems, rather than through the display of abstract and theoretical statements.

It is my pleasant obligation to thank the contributors who took upon themselves the sincere task to present their own scholarship. The result, the diversity in research and focus of interests, created out of the different accords reflects the concert of true and sound scholarship.

Gratitude is expressed to the following for permission to reproduce copyrighted material: Yale University Art Gallery, for Dura Europus Synagogue, *Ezekiel's Vision,* and Edward Hicks's *The Peaceable Kingdom;* Rijksmuseum, for Rembrandt's *Jeremiah;* Boston Public Library for John Singer Sargent's *The Prophets;* and Art Resource, for Michelangelo's *Jonah.*

THE EXPANSION OF PROPHECY IN THE MARI ARCHIVES: NEW TEXTS, NEW READINGS, NEW INFORMATION

Herbert B. Huffmon

1. Introduction

The discoveries at Mari, the old city on the Middle Euphrates, especially the extensive archives from the Old Babylonian period excavated during the 1930's and beyond, have long interested biblical scholars because of the reports on city and village life and customs in the Patriarchal era. The Mari discoveries provided background for various aspects of early Israel's organization and ritual, including what may be called "intuitive prophecy" (Malamat 1989a). The "revelations" about prophecy in the Mari texts really began in 1948, when Georges Dossin published "Une révélation du dieu Dagan à Terqa," reporting a special dream message intended for transmission to the king. This was followed in 1950 by an article by Adolphe Lods, "Une tablette inédite de Mari, intéressante pour l'histoire ancienne du prophétisme sémitique," on the basis of a transcription and translation, with brief commentary, by Dossin. When these texts were combined with a few less dramatic Mari texts that appeared between 1941 and 1950, a new field of study had begun. There was now available some significant information on the early history of prophetic activity in the biblical world. By 1967 the prophetic texts from Mari numbered well over twenty— W. L. Moran translated twenty-three letters for the 1969 edition of *Ancient Near Eastern Texts*. Other texts from Mesopotamia supplemented the Mari information about prophecy prior to the emergence of Israel (Ellis 1987, 1989; Weippert; Huffmon), but the Mari texts have remained predominant.

An extensive scholarly literature was soon available. The older affirmation of biblical prophecy as derivative of the Canaanites, for which there are but few hints, gave way to the evidence for earlier prophetic activity within the Amorite-Akkadian milieu along the Middle Euphrates. The debate concerning the history of Near Eastern prophecy shifted to questions about definition and about continuity or discontinuity with respect to the prophets of Israel. One issue was whether the Mari personnel should be identified as prophets or as prophet-diviners, as including independent, private prophets or as including only cult functionaries. The other issue was whether there was a functional parallel between the Mari figures and the Biblical prophets, given the differences between the two religious systems. Some scholars denied the continuity of the classical prophets even with the "pre-classical" Israelite prophets, not to mention the activity reported in the Mari letters. Scholars did generally acknowledge the connection between the "official" Mari prophets and the cult/court prophets of Israel.

After 1967 new information and new texts became available in dribs and drabs. In 1967 Dossin published the cuneiform copies of the feminine correspondence, which included many prophetic texts. Various translations followed, although Dossin's "official" transcription and translation, in collaboration with André Finet, appeared only in 1978. In addition, in various separate studies between 1948 and 1975, Dossin published—at times only in (partial) translation—six prophetic texts. (Two of these were subsequently joined together [Lafont]!)

Beginning in 1983 the situation changed dramatically. With the energies of a new team led by J.-M. Durand and D. Charpin, thousands of texts—especially administrative and legal texts—have appeared. Then, in 1988, there was an enormous outpouring of new letters, including many prophetic texts and a reediting of virtually all those prophetic texts previously available. These new texts and reeditions are contained in the *Archives Épistolaires de Mari*, I/1–2 (also numbered as *Archives Royales de Mari, XXVI*), by Jean-Marie Durand, Dominique Charpin, Francis Joannès, Sylvie Lackenbacher, and Bertrand Lafont, who published 560 letters in transliteration and translation, with extensive commentary, spread over 1239 quarto pages. Of these letters, 495 are new; the 70 republished letters usually have revised readings, and seven of them even involve new "joins." J.-M. Durand, to whose energy and direction we are greatly indebted, is the principal contributor. By comparison, volumes 1–6 of the *Archives Royales de Mari* (*ARM*) contained 620 letters and appeared over a span from 1941–1953 in cuneiform copy, and 1950–1954 in transliteration and translation. Subsequently, between 1964 and 1978, volumes 10, 13, 14 and 18 of the Mari series contained another 495 letters. The impact of these first two parts of the new "Archives Épistolaires"—a third part is promised soon—is obviously immense.

Part of the impact of this new epistolary material is the careful editorial correlation of the letters with the administrative and legal texts, so as to provide information for the setting and date of individual letters. Also, the editors were able to draw upon extensive files of collations and unpublished material.

2. The Prophetic Corpus

The corpus of letters concerning "prophecy," in the wide sense, has greatly expanded. In addition to the letters gathered together in *AEM* I/1–2, there are three other "prophetic" letters. One previously published letter, A.1121 + A.2731, reports messages from Addu of Aleppo/Addu of Kallassu (Lafont), messages closely related to the report in letter A.1968, published subsequently (Durand 1993). Another more recently published letter, M.13741, refers to activities of some *muhhû*(s) of the deity Amu of Hubshalum (Birot, No. 32). The corpus now numbers over fifty by a moderately generous count. Of these, twenty-six or so are new. For twenty-two of the previously published letters Durand offers important revised readings based on collation of the tablets. Several of these texts, as mentioned, have new "joins." Most of these texts are gathered in the sections "Les textes prophétiques" and "Les rêves," together with a very valuable and lengthy discussion (Durand 1988, 375–452, 453–82; see also Charpin 1992). Another new text, No. 243, one which, curiously, Durand himself does not mention in his discussion of the prophetic texts, appears in the section "Les événements fortuits, indices de la volonté divine" (Durand 1988, 483–506).

The new texts show the "official" prophets, those with special titles, in much more assertive roles than suggested by the texts previously available. The new texts also indicate one revised title and one new title. Also, the pattern of private persons receiving revelations through dreams is underscored.

3. Examples from the New Material

The most dramatic example of new readings following collation is No. 205, actually a text previously published as part of the corpus of metallurgical texts! The text is not well preserved, and half the tablet is altogether lost. One understandable portion is of particular interest:

> Dagan has informed [me], as follows: "I will surely unveil the weapons. I have touched the [forehe]ad of the [ser]va[nts] of Zimri-Lim. I have sent (them) [af]ter [y]ou."

Apart from the startling new reading of the text, No. 205 has a number of interesting elements, including the idiom "touch the forehead," a symbolic gesture involved in a designation or an oath. The process of divine informing is not indicated, but the letter presumably reports a prophetic revelation.

No. 222 is a republication of *ARM* X.106. Although only five signs are read differently, these slight differences, together with accumulated information from other texts and judicious restorations, move this letter into the prophetic corpus. Irra-gamil occurs in this text, and a man of the same name occurs in recently published administrative texts from Mari as a *muhhû,* or "ecstatic," of Nergal. (Intriguingly, an Old Babylonian seal lists another Irra-gamil as "servant of Nergal"; Anbar, 63.) Given these references, the twofold restoration of [X-X-(X)]-(*he-*)*e-em* as *immahêm,* "became ecstatic," is convincing. Durand's reconstruction—he is often rather bold, but this instance is especially attractive—is:

> Speak to Darish-libur. Thus says Usharesh-hetil, your [son]. "[With reference to the daughter o]f the queen, he has [become ecsta]tic. [The daughter of] my lor[d did not live. Today sh]e has die[d]. She was born the 4/6th [day. . . . On that day] Irra-gamil [became ecsta]tic. [Thus h]e spoke: '[She will not li]ve.'

> [Before the ki]ng arrives at Mari, tell him that this daughter is dead. Make sure he knows. [P]erhaps the king might hear of the death of that daughter when he enters Mari, and be concerned (and) be disturbed."

If we draw upon this combination of data, No. 222 would be the first instance in the letters of a *muhhû*, "ecstatic," who is actually described as becoming ecstatic. (There is a previously known reference to such behavior by a *muhhû* in the Ishtar ritual text from Mari, and other categories of persons are also described as becoming ecstatic. So the *muhhû* is not only etymologically an ecstatic.) It is of special interest that the message concerns the king's family affairs. The king, indeed the person of the king, was of central importance. The king is not a private individual, so his response even to rather personal matters is of public concern. Also, given the associations of the gods Irra and Nergal with fever and infectious disease, the "ecstatic's" presumed divine connections are quite striking.

No. 414 represents a "join" effected by D. Charpin with a portion of a letter from Yasim-El to his lord, Zimri-Lim (*ARM* II.108), first published in 1941. The initial portion includes lines 1–8 and 38–42; the newly joined fragment, published with copy, includes lines 5–39. The full text, as edited by J.-M. Durand, provides in its latter part a most fascinating reference to the activity of an *āpilu*, or "answerer," of Shamash, one who acts in a very assertive manner (lines 29–42):

> Moreover, Atamrum, the *āpilu* of Shamash, has come to me and spoken as follows: "Send me a discrete scribe and I will have (him) write down the news which Shamash has sent me for the king." This is what he said to me. (So) I sent Utu-kam and he has written this tablet. Now this man (i.e., Atamrum) has arranged some elders/witnesses, and he spoke to m[e a]s follows: "Send this tablet quic[kly] and let him (i.e., the king) act according to its words." Thus he said to me. Now, I have sent this tablet to my Lord.

Atamrum, a remarkably assertive "answerer," insists upon—and gets—a special scribe to write down his message, a process quite different from the vast majority of messages that were communicated orally to an official who then wrote to the king.

And the "answerer" advises the king to act in accordance with the message. Moreover, as explicitly indicated in some other new texts as well, the prophet communicates the message publicly. There is no indication of reticence, no private audience. (Note that the scribe is apparently chosen with special care. He has a Sumerian name meaning, "He is Utu's," connecting him with the god Utu, the Sumerian counterpart of Shamash.)

It also happens that a letter from an *āpilu* of Shamash was already known, published in (partial) translation only by Dossin in 1966. This letter is now published in full, with photo, as No. 194, with many differences from Dossin's translation. Durand regards No. 194 as the very letter referred to in No. 414.

[Sp]e[ak t]o Z[i]mri-L[im. T]hus says the *āpilu* [o]f [Shama]sh: "Thus says Shamash: '[I am] the Lord of the Lan[d]. The great throne from the dwelling place of [my de]sire, and your daughter whom I requested of you, let them send quickly to Sippar, [cit]y of life.

Now, the kings who [conf]ronted you and [habitually plu]ndered [you] h[ave been pu]t i[n]to your po[we]r.

Now, the . . . has been given [to you i]n the country. And a[s fo]r the taboo material of Ad[du], (concerning which) [I se]nt to you Kanisanum, prior to the defeat, gather up all the forbidden material and [let] them bring (it) [to H]alab, to the temple of Addu.

[The pre]sent for Dagan, [concerning which the *āpi*]*lu* spoke to y[ou]—(or [That which Qi]shti-Dagan, [the *āpi*]*lu*, said to y[ou])—giv[e th]is, [that he may s]end [you] yo[ur . . .] and [your l]ife.

Furthermore, Ner[ga]l, [ki]ng of Hubshalum, stood at your [sid]e and at the side of your forces in the (time of) the defeat (of the enemies). Whatever you dedicated, and a great bronze sword, have (it) made and let them bring (it all) to Nergal, [k]ing of Hubshalum.'

And furthermore, thus says Shamash: 'Hammu-rapi, king of Kurda, has sp[oken] deceptive (words) with you, and his hand is placed somewhere else. Your hand will [overcome him] and you will give fr[ee rein] to an edict of restoration in [his] country. And now, a[ll] the land is give[n] into your hand. When you sei[ze] the city and give free rein to an edict of restoration, [s]o your kingship will be [pe]rpetu[al].

And furthermore, let Zimri-Lim, the viceroy of D[agan] and Addu, hear this ta[ble]t, and let him sen[d] to my feet (anyone with) a [cl]aim.'"

This letter was one of the early indications of the more assertive role of the Mari prophets, a feature that has emerged much more clearly in the new texts. Also striking is the way in which this letter from the *āpilu* of Shamash includes requests also for three other deities—Addu, Dagan and Nergal—and relates to a wide geographical range of cultic activity. Sippar, a central Babylonian city associated especially with Shamash, is mentioned, as is Halab/Aleppo in the west. The "answerer" also reinforces the message of a colleague, if the restorations are correct. In the conclusion, the message reverts to Shamash, lord of justice, who asserts his leadership by asking the king to send to him anyone with a dispute.

One of the most surprising new letters is No. 206, reporting rather strange activity by a *muhhû* (an "ecstatic"), strange, perhaps, even when compared to the symbolic acts of Israel's prophets.

> Sp[eak] to [my Lord]. Thus says [Yaqqim-Addu], [your] servant. A *muhhû* [of Dagan] came to me and th[us] he [spoke]: "Cer[tainly] I will eat [something] of Zi[mri-Lim's]. [Give (me)] a la[mb] and let me eat (it)."
>
> [I gave] him a lamb and he ate it raw [i]n [fr]ont of the Gate. And he assembled the elders in front of the Sagaratum Gate, and this is what he said: "Pestilence is at hand; summon the <c>ities; let them return the forbidden material. A man who makes an assault, let them expel (him) from the city. And, for the well-being of your Lord, Zi[mri-Lim], you should clothe me with a garment."
>
> This is what he said to me, so for the well-being of [my] Lord, I clot[hed him] with a garment. Now, the me[ssage which] he spoke to [me, I have written down and] I have sent (it) to [my Lord]. Now, he did not speak his message in secret (?), (but) he gave his message in the assembly of the elders.

The eating of a lamb is doubtless a symbolic act akin to actions mentioned in curses, so it evokes here some unspecified prior claim which is now going to be enforced by the deity, presumably Dagan. Note the curse invoked on malefactors in the Ashur-nirari treaty, "May they eat the flesh of their sons (and) their daughters and may it taste as good to them as the flesh of a ram or sheep," and the similar curse in the later Esarhaddon treaty, "Just as this ewe is cut open and the flesh of its young placed in its mouth, so may he (Shamash?) make you eat in your hunger the flesh of your brothers, your sons, and your daughters" (Hillers 62–63). As further instances of assertiveness, the *muhhû* assembles the elders at one of the city gates as witnesses and demands a garment from the king's official. Illustrating such activity, the recently published administrative texts have many examples of the distribution to "answerers" and "ecstatics" of garments, silver and bronze items, and even in one instance a donkey (e.g., Durand, 1988, 380–81, 396–97). The status of the prophets is such that Durand views them as essentially official messengers (Durand, 1988, 380).

A striking occurrence in the new texts is the earliest clear example of the title *nāb(i')u/nābû* as an etymological correlate of Hebrew *nābî'*, "prophet." (The citations from the Ebla texts are later and rather more complicated.) The text is No. 216:

> Speak to my Lord: Thus says Tebi-geri-shu, your servant. "The day after I reached Ashmad, I assembled the *nābûs* (LÚ *na-bi-i*.MEŠ) of the Hanaeans. I had an omen taken for the well-being of my Lord: 'Will my Lord, when he makes [his ab]lutions and [st]ays for 7 days ou[tside (the city)], [return] safely [to the ci]ty?' . . . [6–8 lines lost]
>
> When [my Lord goes to (the temple of) Annunitum], outside (the city), may my Lord take care of [hi]mself. [Let the troops be at readiness] for [my] Lord, and strengt[hen] the [city's] guard. Let my Lord not be neglectful of [him]self."

Tebi-geri-shu, a palace official known in other texts, visits a certain Ashmad, who is elsewhere associated with the Hanaeans. He then assembles the *nābûs* and presents them with a typical binary divination inquiry, a situation that parallels 1 Kings 22. The text as preserved provides no further information about the activity of the *nābûs*, although we may assume that they provided an answer to the question. (The title is also now attested in the somewhat later texts from Emar. Although the function in those texts seems even less clear, the focus may be upon invoking the gods; see Fleming.) In terms of what the text tells us, the *nābûs* function in a way similar to the technical diviner, just as the prophetic group—and Micaiah—in 1 Kings 22 parallel priestly divination with the sacred lots. We have, then, a further link in the prehistory of biblical prophecy and a reminder of how functions change over the centuries. Continuity of title is not the same as continuity of function.

The texts offer yet another new title, in the sense that a title formerly generally read as *qabbātu*, "(f.) speaker," is now read *qam(m)atu*. Collation of the first occurrence, in No. 197 (*ARM* X.80), combined with new examples in No. 199 (both written 1 SAL *qa-ma-tum*) and No. 203 (written [SAL *qa]-am-ma- [tim]*), indicate the title is *qam(m)atu*, but the title is of uncertain derivation. It may have to do with "arise" (Northwest Semitic *qum*), although Durand suggests a reference to a special hairdo (cf. Akk. *qamāmu/qimmatu*; Durand 1988, 396). An intriguing element in the letters involved is that in two of the three instances the *qam(m)atu* of Dagan of Terqa quotes the proverb, "Beneath the straw water flows"—a proverb that is also cited in No. 202, apparently as spoken by a *muhhû* (of Dagan). The proverb is surely used of the deceptive behavior of the realm of Eshnunna.

Another new text is a striking illustration of a "double" revelation. In No. 227, a letter from Addu-duri, a very important woman at the court of Mari, perhaps even the queen mother, we learn of a revelatory speech by third parties within a woman's dream:

[Speak to my Lord. Thus says] (lady) Addu-duri. "(Lady) [X-b]ilau [has se]en a dream. This is what she said: '[In] my [dre]am [Ha]dnu-El [and] Iddin-Kubi, *[m]uhhûs*, we[re] a[li]ve and went in to be with (the god) Abba. This is what they said: "Speak (f.pl.) to (the spirits of) your (f.pl.) stillborn children (*ku-bi-ki-na*), and let Zimri-Lim make a harvest of well-being. [Z]im[ri-L]im . . . [6–7 lines lost]

The intimation of the text is that two deceased "ecstatics" (Durand 1988, 397) make an appearance. The cult of the dead is prominent at Mari, but this is a unique text—dead "ecstatics," dead children. It is also a revelation at one remove. Yet the *muhhûs* speak with one voice in a dream of lady [X-b]ilau, speaking as it were with divine authority. Her dream is then reported to the king by a highly placed court lady. Note that one of the *muhhûs* has a name recognizing the numen of the deified stillborn child, Kubu. In their message, it is not clear just who is supposed to speak. It may be the child-bearing women of Mari in general, or it may be the palace women in particular.

Text No. 237 (*ARM* X.50) reports on an apparent dream in which a *šangû*, an administrative priest, repeatedly utters a curious cry ("Turn/Return, O Dagan"). But text No. 227 is the clearest example of a revelatory prophetic speech within a dream or vision.

The report of revelatory speeches by persons within dreams raises the issue of authority. It suggests that dreams were subordinate in authority to prophetic revelations, insofar as the revelatory role in dreams commonly filled by a deity is filled by (deceased) prophetic speakers, themselves presumably speaking for the god Abba. Dreams that report messages from deities or authorized figures surely were taken quite seriously.

Recently Durand (1993) published another report of prophetic activity at Halab/Aleppo. A.1968, a letter to Zimri-Lim sent by his emissary at Halab, Nur-Sin, and rather reminiscent of A.1121 + A.2731 (Lafont), is especially interesting:

> Speak to my lord. Thus says Nur-Sin, your servant: Abiya, the *āpilu* of Addu, lord of Hala[b], came to me and spoke as follows: Thus says Addu: I have given the land in its entirety to Yahdu(n)-Lim. And due to my weapons, he had no equal. (Yet) he abandoned what was mine and the country which I had given to hi[m] I have [gi]ven to Samsi-Addu . . . [10 or so lines lost]
>
> . . . let me re[sto]re you. To the th[rone of your father's house] I restored you. The weapon[s] with which I fought with the Sea I have given to you. With the oil of my splendor I have anointed you and no one has sto[od] up to you. Hear my one [w]ord: Whenever anyone with a claim cries out to <you>, saying, 'I have been w[rong]ed,' stand up and decide his case; ans[wer him fai]rly. [T]hat is what I [desire] of you. When you [go forth] on a campaign, do not [go forth wi]thout an oracle. [W]hen in m[y] or[a]cle I become manifest, go forth on campaign. [I]f it is [not s]o, you should [not] go out the gate.
>
> This is what the *āpilu* said to me. Now [, the hair of the *āpilu*] and [his] h[em, I have had sent to my lord.]

On the historical side, the shift of Addu's support from Yahdun-Lim, "father" of Zimri-Lim, to his rival, Samsi-Addu of Assyria, and then back to Zimri-Lim, underscores the importance of divine favor. Indeed, it is especially noteworthy when the divine favor comes from the one who battled the Sea, whose triumphant weapons are now given to Zimri-Lim. No wonder that Addu, as in A.1121 + (Lafont), holds the king to a special standard of justice, using language reminiscent of the epilogue of Hammu-rapi's famous stele.

The new corpus has many other treasures. In some instances our limited information is most tantalizing. The increasing variety of activity and titles shows us something of a time in which a wide range of means of divine communication was possible. With the occurrence of the title *nābû* among the Hanaeans, the connection with the later biblical *nābî'* is now more direct (Fleming).

4. Mari and Israel

Obviously there is a temporal and geographical gap between the Mari texts and early Israel, even though the range of the Mari evidence for prophecy reaches to Aleppo, and even though Zimri-Lim once even paid a visit to Ugarit. (Also, his wife Yatar-aya may well have hailed from Hazor.) It clearly is not a matter of direct continuity. Nonetheless, the Mari activity does provide a phenomenological background for biblical prophecy, both in the cultic and the non-cultic forms. Biblical prophecy can now be seen as part of an ancient and honorable history of such activity in Greater Syria and as an instance of the wider phenomenology of prophetic mediation for the divine realm. As the new Mari texts make clear, that ancient story includes bold, assertive actions by the prophets, as well as very dramatic, even flamboyant, symbolic acts. The messages—predominantly oracles of assurance but also admonitions and indictments of foreign powers—are usually brief, yet some are comparatively lengthy.

The new Mari texts also continue to illustrate both official, cultic prophecy and private or individual prophecy. (For the latter category, dreams predominate.) It is interesting that in addition to reassurance to the king and material requests, there are admonitions of the king. The boldest admonitions of the king—for cultic failure and for the necessity to uphold the highest standards of justice as well—come from those "professional" prophets associated with specific deities, not from private persons. From these prophets, contrary to the dominant Mesopotamian tradition and in similarity to Israel, there does seem to be "evidence testifying to the existence of an autonomous elite that could criticize the king's equity or question his righteousness" (contra Tadmor, 217, see also 224), righteousness seen especially in cultic terms. (Granted, some—but not all—of the admonitions are from deities whose shrines are outside the range of Zimri-Lim's control. The related evidence from extispicy [George, 18–23] could be viewed as indirect or after the event.) Also striking is the increasing evidence of a wide, public audience. In the previously published texts the prophets might at times address not only the king but, for example, the citizens of Terqa; in the new texts they also occasionally summon the elders and speak to a public assembly. These prophets appear as inspired speakers on behalf of the divine realm, not only as courtiers of the king. With the new texts, the phenomenological parallel between Mari prophecy and biblical prophecy is more impressive than before. As an extra, the most common biblical title, *nābî*, has a prehistory in Syria. It is not new, but an old, if minor, title.

To be sure, biblical religion differs from the religion of the Amorite provinces of Mesopotamia, and Mari prophecy differs from biblical prophecy. Phenomenologically, however, the parallel is clear, and that is the proper point of comparison. One cannot require identity in detail; that would mean virtually an equation of the religious world of the Mari prophets and that of biblical Israel. Granted, the uniqueness of Israel is frequently overstated—note the similar problem in dealing with Early Christianity (Smith, 36–53, 116–18)—yet it is clear that the Mari prophets in their world are not a match for Jeremiah, however reconstructed. (But is it fair to set the brief period for which Mari prophecy is attested—perhaps 14 years—over against the whole history of prophecy in Israel?)

The Mari evidence is a wonderful resource for the history of prophecy. Clearly the range of evidence now available creates problems for those who would stress any large-scale uniqueness of Israelite prophecy or for those who would argue for a comparatively late date for the development of "real" prophecy in

Israel. Already, prompted by the new material, many important new connections have been explored (see Malamat 1989b, 1991a, 1991b, 1993; Parker; Barstad). Those interested in the history of prophecy may expect a number of new studies to supplement the extensive literature that existed previous to the 1988 publications (Malamat 1989a, 79–96, 125–44).

Future studies of the history of prophecy have a very rich resource in the expanded Mari corpus. We are greatly indebted to J.-M. Durand and D. Charpin and their colleagues for their work on these marvelous texts. We look forward to additional treasures.

Works Consulted

Anbar, M.

1976   "Trois documents de la collection Leo Perutz." *Israel Oriental Studies* 6:59–64, with 2 plates.

Barstad, H. M.

1993   "No Prophets? Recent Developments in Biblical Prophetic Research and Ancient Near Eastern Prophecy." *JSOT* 57:39–60.

Birot, M.

1993   *Correspondance des gouverneurs de Qaṭṭunân*. Archives Royales de Mari XXVII. Paris: Éditions Recherche sur les Civilisations.

Charpin, D.

1992   "Le contexte historique et géographique des prophéties dans les textes retrouvés à Mari." *Bulletin, The Canadian Society for Mesopotamian Studies* 23:21–31.

Charpin, D. et al.

1988   *Archives Épistolaires de Mari I/2*. Archives Royales de Mari XXVI. Paris: Éditions Recherche sur les Civilisations.

Dossin, G.

1948   "Une révélation du dieu Dagan à Terqa." *Revue d'assyriologie* 42:125–34.

1966   "Sur le prophétisme à Mari." Pp. 77–86 in *La divination en Mésopotamie ancienne* (XIVe Rencontre Assyriologique internationale). Paris: Presses universitaires de France.

Durand, J.-M.

1988   *Archives Épistolaires de Mari I/1*. Archives Royales de Mari XXVI. Paris: Éditions Recherche sur les Civilisations.

1993   "Le mythologème du combat entre le Dieu de l'orage et la Mer en Mésopotamie." *MARI* 7:41–61.

Ellis, M. deJ.

1987   "The Goddess Kititum Speaks to King Ibalpiel: Oracle Texts from Ishchali." *MARI* 5:235–66.

1989   "Observations on Mesopotamian Oracles and Prophetic Texts: Literary and Historiographic Considerations." *JCS* 41:127–86.

Fleming, D. E.

1993   "The Etymological Origins of the Hebrew *nābîʾ*: The One Who Invokes God." *CBQ* 55:217–24.

George, L.

1990   "Mesopotamian Extispicy: Explorations in Ethics and Metaphysics." *Bulletin, The Canadian Society for Mesopotamian Studies* 19:15–24.

Hillers, D. R.

1964   *Treaty Curses and the Old Testament Prophets*. Biblica et Orientalia, 16. Rome: Pontifical Biblical Institute.

Huffmon, H. B.

1992   "Ancient Near Eastern Prophecy." Pp. 477–82 in *The Anchor Bible Dictionary*, vol. 5, ed. D. N. Freedman et al. New York: Doubleday.

Lafont, B.

1984   "Le roi de Mari et les prophètes du dieu Adad." *RA* 78:7–18.

Lods, A., with G. Dossin

1950   "Un tablette inédite de Mari, intérresante pour l'histoire ancienne du prophétisme sémitique." Pp. 103–10 in *Studies in Old Testament Prophecy Presented to Professor Theodore H. Robinson*, ed. H. H. Rowley. New York: Scribner's.

Malamat, A.

1989a   *Mari and the Early Israelite Experience*. The Schweich Lectures of the British Academy, 1984. Oxford: Oxford University Press.

1989b   "Parallels between the New Prophecies from Mari and Biblical Prophecy: I) Predicting the Death of a Royal Infant"; "II) Material Remuneration for Prophetic Services," *Nouvelles Assyriologiques Brèves et Utilitaires* 61–64 (nos. 88–89).

1991a   "New Light from Mari (ARM XXVI) on Biblical Prophecy (III-IV)." Pp. 185–90 in *Storia e tradizioni di Israele. Scritti in onore di J. Alberto Soggin*, ed. D. Garrone and F. Israel. Brescia: Paideia.

1991b   "The Secret Council and Prophetic Involvement in Mari and Israel." Pp. 231–36 in *Prophetie und geschichtliche Wirklichkeit im alten Israel. Festschrift für Siegfried Wagner zum 65. Geburtstag*, ed. R. Liwak and S. Wagner. Stuttgart: Kohlhammer.

1993   "A New Prophetic Message from Aleppo and Its Biblical Counterparts." Pp. 236–41 in *Understanding Poets and Prophets. Essays in Honour of George Wishart*

Anderson, ed. A. G. Auld. JSOTSup 152. Sheffield: Sheffield Academic.

Parker, S. B.
1993   "Official attitudes toward prophecy at Mari and in Israel." *VT* 43:50–68.

Sasson, J. M.
1994   "The Posting of Letters with Divine Messages." Pp. 299–316 in *Florilegium marianum II. Recueil d'études à la mémoire de Maurice Birot*, ed. D. Charpin and J.-M. Durand. Mémoires de N.A.B.U., 3. Paris: SEPOA.

Smith, J. Z.
1990   *Drudgery Divine. On the Comparison of Early Christianities and the Religions of Late Antiquity.* Chicago: University of Chicago.

Tadmor, H.
1986   "Monarchy and the Elite in Assyria and Babylonia: The Question of Royal Accountability." Pp. 203–24 in *The Origins and Diversity of Axial Age Civilizations*, ed. S. Eisenstadt. Albany: State University of New York.

Weippert, M.
1988   "Aspekte israelitischer Prophetie im Lichte verwandter Erscheinungen des Alten Orients." Pp. 287–319 in *Ad bene et fideliter seminandum. Festgabe für Karlheinz Deller zum 21. Februar 1987.* Kevelaer: Butzon und Bercker; Neukirchen-Vluyn: Neukirchener.

Rethinking the Nature
of Prophetic Literature

David L. Petersen

Both the phrase, "The Prophets," when used as a category with which to subsume a major portion of the Hebrew Bible canon, and the phrase, "the prophetic literature," have proven to be surprisingly ambiguous over the centuries. As a rubric, "The Prophets" has been variously applied to include everything in the Hebrew Bible other than the Pentateuch or to "just" the former and latter prophets; and "the prophetic literature" has been applied sometimes to books titled with a prophet's name, sometimes to narratives embedded in the deuteronomistic history, e.g., the Elijah stories, and sometimes to texts located in non-prophetic biblical books, e.g., the oracles of Balaam, which occur in the Pentateuch. In sum, one may well ask, what are "The Prophets?" and what is "prophetic literature?" In this paper, I shall focus on the latter of these two questions.

There is no obvious and compelling answer. Moreover, the current state of biblical studies with its new patterns of research has exacerbated the problem. Debate continues over the value of various higher critical perspectives, e.g., form or redaction criticism. And within the last two decades, various social and literary perspectives (in some cases quite without relevant knowledge of appropriate research have been added to the methodological stew).[1] So, what critical perspectives are

---

[1] Instead of citing uninformed treatments, I prefer to point to work that is of special value for those undertaking a literary approach. For example, discussion of the book of Jeremiah from a literary perspective should take account of the work of Diamond (1990) on characterization, which itself represents a careful comparison between the LXX and MT literary presentations. Or, study of the book of Isaiah as a meaningful literary unit should be informed by recourse to the redaction critical analysis of those like Sweeney, Vermeylen or Williamson.

appropriate for addressing this question concerning the nature of prophetic literature?

In addressing these issues, I propose a five-fold typology for prophetic literature and comment briefly on its implications. This typology derives, in part, from an assessment of the diverse forms of prophetic behavior, better said, intermediation, in ancient Israel, and in part from the study of literature that reflects the activities or perspectives of these intermediaries (Wilson). In turn, I will examine a number of assumptions regarding prophetic literature, which do not take account either of the just-mentioned diversity or of other salient features of Israel's prophetic literature. In sum, I will employ various critical perspectives in order to understand fundamental features of prophetic literature.

I

In an earlier study (Petersen, 1981), I argued that the Hebrew Bible presents four role labels that reflect diverse forms of prophecy in ancient Israel (see now Moore, 1990a, 1990b). The role labels are *ḥōzeh, rōʾeh, nābîʾ,* and *ʾîš hāʾĕlōhîm.* The first two are normally translated "seer," the third, "prophet," and the fourth, "man of God." Although over time the third term, *nābîʾ,* achieved primacy as *the* term for prophet, these four role labels point to moments in Israel's history when not all intermediaries were known as *nĕbîʾîm;* they point to situations in which not all intermediaries did the same thing, and they point to periods when intermediaries at the same time acted in diverse ways.

As a corollary, it is appropriate to think that differing kinds of prophetic activity normally resulted in different kinds of literature. As a result, I will explore the four role labels mentioned above as something like Weberian ideal types. By using the notion of ideal types, I mean to suggest that one type of intermediary may be characterized by a certain kind of activity, but that behavior of another sort may be present as well. In addition, one kind of literature will be especially prominent for a particular type of prophetic behavior.

A. *rōʾeh,* "seer." Though one may translate this Hebrew noun accurately with the word "seer," the use of this word in the Hebrew

Bible suggests that the *rō'eh* exercised a role different from that of
the *ḥōzeh*. One may view the *rō'eh* type prophet as something akin to
a diviner. If the term *rō'eh* refers to a kind of diviner, as 1 Sam 9:9,
11 suggest, then we would expect a certain sort of literature to
reflect divinatory or prophetic consultative activity (Overholt:117–
47). One often thinks of divination as mechanical. However, there
are a number of instances in the Hebrew Bible in which individuals
request information from a prophet and in which they receive an
oral response without any indication that mechanical divination
(e.g., Urim and Thummim) had been used.[2]

Such forms of intermediation involve social interaction in ways
not always evident in other forms of prophetic activity.[3] The
intermediary has an audience, which itself takes the initiative in
seeking information from the deity (e.g., Ezek 20:1). Literature
attesting to this form of prophecy will almost inevitably be written
as a prose chronicle or narrative. That narrative may focus on the
information garnered by divination or it may report the process of
social interaction, as is the case in 1 Samuel 9. Here the literature
normally does more than simply present the request for divinatory
perspective; and it does more than preserve or record the
utterance of the intermediary.[4] The interaction of the intermediary
with the audience, apart from the divinatory utterance, is itself part
of the standard behavior of that prophet (as Jer 38:14–28
demonstrates). Hence, literature attesting to that larger complex
of interaction should be construed as prophetic literature.

Apart from the case of Samuel, who is appelled *rō'eh* (1 Sam
9:9, 11), the Hebrew Bible includes other instances in which a
prophet, not labelled *rō'eh*, performs this consultative role. Ezekiel
20 presents a scene in which the prophet, living in exile, received
representatives from "the elders of Israel." They had come to

---

[2] Some Mari texts, e.g., *ARM* X,4, in which an individual submits a request
to an intermediary, may be classified as this kind of prophetic literature. Cf. H.
B. Huffmon's article in this volume.

[3] See Overholt:17–25 on the importance of recognizing that prophecy
involves social interaction, not simply isolated verbal utterance.

[4] In contrast, the Neo-Assyrian divinatory texts present only the request for
information, e.g., text #12 in Starr.

"inquire from Yahweh."[5] Yahweh speaks through the prophet and responds to the elders (though in terms they had not anticipated). Balaam, a non-Israelite prophet, provides a second case. He is approached, with "divination fees" (Num 22:7) in the hands of the representatives of Balak the Moabite king, to pronounce a curse upon Israel. After apparently accepting the fees, Balaam is initially forbidden from undertaking the requested divination.

Finally, the most straightforward case of a prophet receiving a request for a divine oracle and then providing the expected response occurs in Zechariah 7–8. Again, there are representatives sent. The citizenry of Bethel empowered legates to ask priests and prophets in Jerusalem, "Should I mourn and fast in the fifth month . . . ?" (Zech 7:3). The prophet responds: "The fast of the fourth month, and the fast of the fifth, and the fast of the seventh, and the fast of the tenth, shall be to the house of Judah seasons of joy and gladness." (Zech 8:19). The prophet provides a wide-ranging negative answer for the emissaries: there are to be no more lamentations of that sort.

In these and other cases (e.g., Jeremiah and Zedekiah [Jer 38:14]), prophetic literature attests to interaction between the intermediary and those who want information from the deity. The deity's response, which is communicated by the prophet, is only one, though important, part of the larger literary complex. The prophet as divinatory speaker is clearly attested in one kind of prophetic literature, the divinatory chronicle.

B. *ḥōzeh*, "seer." The noun, "seer," figures prominently in several Judahite prophetic books, i.e., Amos (7:12), Isaiah (29:10; 30:9–10), and Micah (3:5–8). And it is surely not coincidental that visions, *ḥezyōnōt*—or, more precisely stated, vision reports—occur in these books. The vocabulary of visions is prominent even in the editorial formulae, e.g., Isa 1:1, "the vision of Isaiah the son of Amoz, which he saw concerning . . . ;" Isa 2:1, "the word which Isaiah the son of Amoz saw concerning . . . ;" Hab 1:1, "The oracle which Habakkuk the prophet saw." Since ancient Israelite writers

---

[5] The verb *dāraš* here and elsewhere (e.g., 1 Kgs 22:5) signifies a request for a divine oracle.

themselves identified some intermediaries as "seers," e.g., Gad, as David's "seer" (2 Sam 24:11), one has *prima facie* grounds for thinking that literature involving visions may be associated with intermediaries who are "visionaries." And such is the case.

Vision reports have been the subject of numerous important articles and monographic length treatments. For the purposes of this study, it is important to recognize that vision reports are often formulated in a stereotypic manner (Sister, 1934; Horst, 1960; Jeremias, 1977). Moreover, there seems to have been a tradition in which a series of visions are reported, e.g., Amos' five visions (Amos 7:1–9; 8:1–3; 9:1–4), Ezekiel's four visions (which begin in 1:1; 8:1; 37:1; 40:1, respectively), Zechariah's eight visions (chaps. 1–6). Unlike the divinatory chronicle or utterance, these visions do not appear to derive from direct solicitation by an audience, though they may have resulted from intentional behavior by the intermediary, e.g., incubation.[6]

However, my contention involving the vision report is "stronger" than standard form-critical arguments. The vision report is often included in catalogues of *Gattungen* that a prophet might use to proclaim a message from the deity (e.g., March, 1974:170). And it may be that some vision reports represent self-conscious rhetorical ploys (e.g., Jer 1:11–15). Nonetheless, it seems probable that the vision reports of Amos, Isaiah, Ezekiel and Zechariah do, in fact, constitute reports of visionary or trance-like experiences. Hence, one should think that Zechariah, in creating his vision reports, is not choosing one among several different literary forms in which to report his experiences and messages. One might think that Amos or Micah had the option of selecting diatribe, lawsuit or judgment oracle to convey a message of admonition or judgment. But the vision report is quite a different matter. This literary form exists as a direct expression of the intermediary as a *ḥōzeh* or visionary. From this perspective, the

---

[6] The practice of incubation—sleeping in a holy place in order to secure a divinatory dream—is attested in the Hebrew Bible, e.g., Solomon (1 Kgs 3:4–5). This issue, however, raises the vexing distinction between dreams and visions or, to use the vocabulary from ancient Greece, waking and sleeping visions, cf. Gen 46:2, "visions of the night."

vision report is a fundamental form of prophetic literature,
attesting to one identifiable type of intermediation, that of
visionary behavior.

C. *nābîʾ*, "prophet." The ideal type associated with this role
label involves auditory perception and utterance by the prophet.
Jeremiah's call narrative (Jer 1:4–10) is salutary. To be a prophet is
to hear Yahweh's word, to have that word placed in one's mouth,
and to utter that word to others. Many Israelite and Judahite
prophets, particularly after the schism that created those two
nations and before the defeat of Judah, acted in ways that allow us
to understand them as a *nābîʾ*.

Various forms of utterance characterize this form of prophetic
behavior. One may say that direct speech is a hallmark (Tucker,
1978). These prophets were speakers, and their utterances were of
two basic types: divine oracles, in which the deity speaks in the first
person (Hosea 11:1–7); and prophetic sayings, in which the
prophet speaks in the first person and refers to Yahweh in the third
person (e.g., Mic 3:5–8). However, since admixtures of these two
forms occur, and with some regularity, one should not construe
them as fundamentally different in rhetorical force. Together,
these two forms of discourse—divine oracle and prophetic saying—
make up the majority of prophetic literature.

Form critical analysis of prophetic literature has helped us to
appreciate the remarkable formal diversity in the speeches of *nābîʾ*
intermediaries. Prophetic speakers exercised great latitude in the
ways they formulated their utterances. They used genres otherwise
attested in the lawcourt, school, and ritual setting, as well as in
everyday speech to configure their discourse. Nonetheless, some
genres occurred with remarkable frequency, e.g., the so-called
announcement of judgment (Westermann, 1967).

D. *ʾîš hāʾĕlōhîm*, "man of God." This phrase occurs most
frequently with reference to the prophets Elisha and Elijah. They
are "holy men," who possess the power of the sacred. They
function as intermediaries neither by saying words from the deity
nor by "seeing into" the divine world. Rather, they themselves
personify the world of the sacred in the profane, but without the

ritual requirements associated with priests, who occupy a similar position on the boundary between the sacred and the profane.

Alexander Rofé has argued convincingly that the stories associated with these holy men form a special type of literature. They are best understood as legends. In a classic form-critical argument, he observed that the *Sitz im Leben* of such stories is the telling of tales about the power of these people by circles of disciples (so 2 Kgs 8:4). Here, if the literature focusing on these figures may be construed as prophetic literature, then it has *reportage* as one of its hallmarks. These are narratives written by someone other than the "holy man;" and these stories essentially celebrate his power. This literature deserves to be understood as prophetic literature, since it attests to and derives from the exercise of one kind of prophetic activity.

E. The fifth and final element in this typology derives from individuals who bear no explicit prophetic title. Mari texts attest such people who receive revelations through dreams (so Huffmon). Similarly, I propose that at least one type of Hebrew Bible literature may derive from untitled intermediaries. We do not know the names or titles of those who wrote the prophetic speeches, stories or comments embedded in the deuteronomistic history. Yet these individuals wrote from a perspective that valued highly the prophetic word. These authors testify to the power of individual prophets (e.g., 1 Kgs 12:15) or to the prophets in general (e.g., "his servants the prophets" [2 Kgs 24:2]). We might label these individuals as prophetic historians, who may be responsible for the prophetic source or redaction evident in parts of the deuteronomistic history. Moreover, we hear impressionistic echoes of such individuals in the Chronicler's history (e.g., 1 Chr 29:29). These references allude to a style of intermediation in the form of history writing.

In sum, a brief review of basic prophetic roles and the literature typically associated with them demonstrates that one ought to expect diversity within the general category "prophetic literature." Moreover, one may discern a five-fold typology: divinatory chronicle, vision report, prophetic speech, legend, and prophetic history. However, there is no simple correlation between prophets known by a particular role label and a certain form or style of literature.[7] As a result, one may envision an individual prophet, e.g., Amos, both reporting visions and offering divine oracles. Similarly, Elijah may be construed as a holy man and a prophetic speaker. One prophet could engage in varied forms of prophetic activity. As a result, prophetic books may include diverse forms of prophetic literature, e.g., vision report and prophetic speech as in Amos.

II

The implications of this typology are far reaching and should affect significantly the ways in which we think about prophetic literature. Diversity within prophetic literature is not commonly recognized, however, because a number of powerful prejudgments operate when people think about the concept of prophetic literature, or, for that matter, prophecy. I list here the most important of such prejudgments and the reasons why they should be reconsidered.

First, some scholars think the prophets acted primarily as formal speakers. The implication here is that prophets were not prophets when they were silent, or when they acted out that which they were required to do, or when they were engaged in conversation. The most serious problem with this view is that it discounts writing as an exercise of a prophet's role. The notion of *Schriftprophetie* is clearly attested in the Hebrew Bible, e.g., Isa 8:16. Moreover, the recent works of authors as diverse as Wiklander (1984), Davis (1989), and Utzschneider (1989), suggest that, rather than being an aberration or a late devolution, intermediation via writing was an appropriate form of prophetic activity. It was even a necessary strategy in certain situations. Prophets could be writers as well as speakers.

There is a corollary to this prejudgment, namely, some presume that the prophets as formal speakers were trying to

---

[7] Cf. Gitay (1989:80), "The prophetic 'oratorical rhetoric,' which has a poetic flavor, is not just a reflection of the prophet's traditional socio-religious role; the prophetic style is a product of their concrete aim."

convince the people to do something, viz., that they were offering a message of repentance. This view has been successfully challenged by a number of scholars (e.g., Tucker, 1987). Some of the prophets were interested in communicating with large numbers of people. However, their messages, as was true for their earlier counterparts at Mari, or their contemporary Balaam at Deir ʿAlla, often involved "fixed" messages, e.g., they reported what was about to happen or why something was to happen.

Second, some scholars assume prophetic literature preserves that which prophets wrote or spoke. They claim that prophetic literature preserves the words, writings, even thoughts of the individual prophet. This claim represents, essentially, a judgment about the "historicity" of the prophetic literature. According to these views, prophets are, ultimately, authors (e.g., Jeffrey, 284–85). Such a judgment will have (and often has had) the effect of presuming or arguing that a given prophetic oracle was, indeed, spoken by the prophet to whom it has been attributed.

However, this notion presents one overly simple answer to a complex question: what is the relation of a prophet to the literature associated with him or her? The prophet as author of that literature is only one among several answers. An amanuensis, a circle of disciples, a later redactor—any of these could serve as author of prophetic literature. Of the five basic types of prophetic literature adumbrated above, the divinatory chronicle and the legend regularly convey the prophet in third person discourse. Here, it is fundamentally inappropriate to think about the prophet as author.

The situation is different for the seer and speaker types. Freedman's assessment of the book of Micah may serve as a case in point: "We will assume that the text is . . . a faithful reproduction of what the prophet said, or what he or, more likely his scribe or editor wrote down" (1983:144). In either case, the term "prophetic" depends upon the presumption that the text provides an eye-witness to, or preserves the words of, the prophet. The use of the term "prophetic" involves, essentially, an historical judgment. Freedman thinks, "we seem to have the raw product straight from the soul of the prophet . . ." (1983:157).

Given this kind of a perception, it is not surprising that a number of scholars have resisted, by way of assumption or argument, the conclusions of other scholars that certain portions of a book ascribed to an individual prophet may be attributed to later authors or editors. The current scholarly climate, with frequent appeals to reading biblical literature in its final or canonical form, enhances this tendency. Nonetheless, questions about the formation of prophetic literature remain foundational. They cannot be assumed away. Recent research regarding the formation of prophetic books offers numerous cases in point (see note 1 above).

Third, some scholars maintain prophets were, essentially, poets. By extension, they suggest prophetic literature should normally be understood as poetry. This sentiment typically involves more than a statistical judgment, viz., much in prophetic books is written in poetry. Instead, those who advocate this notion often speak of a poetic spirit or about inspiration as the source for prophetic activity and, by extension, prophetic literature. Abraham Heschel (1962) provided a classic exposition of this position, e.g., "The prophet is a poet" (147), "Prophecy is poetry" (148). More recently, David Noel Freedman's claims are typical: "poetry and prophecy in the biblical tradition share so many of the same features and overlap to such an extent that one cannot be understood except in terms of the other . . . the correlation between poetry and prophecy. . . . Poetry was the central medium of prophecy" (Freedman, 1977:21–23).[8]

Some interpreters moderate the claim about an integral association of poetry with prophecy by observing that prophetic

---

[8] In a variation on this theme, Freedman has addressed the topic of "prophetic discourse" and maintained that it can occur either as "ordinary narrative or declarative prose," as "poetry in the classic mode," or "an admixture" (1983:141–42). However, one normally associates the term "discourse" with speech, thus making it difficult to describe narrative prose as discourse. Moreover, as Freedman develops his argument, he observes that "prophetic discourse" simply overmaps the three basic sorts of linguistic expression known in the Hebrew Bible, namely, prose, poetry and a mixture of the two, in which case the "prophetic" character is no longer analytically significant.

literature can be written in prose, but they suggest such prose is so infrequent or "prosaic" as to be unimportant. In contrast, Alter has correctly discerned the importance and significance of biblical prose prophetic literature (137–39). Alter argues, and I agree, that prophetic prose may be understood not as a chronological devolution but as a conscious literary and rhetorical strategy (cf. Berlin: 114–15).

To be sure, considerable prophetic literature is written as poetry (N.B., in the NRSV there is more poetry than there was in the RSV [cf. the two translations of Ezekiel 7]). It was to Lowth's credit that he discerned this distinctive feature in much of the prophetic literature. Nonetheless, as I demonstrated in the first portion of this paper, four fundamental forms of prophetic literature are written in prose. And, as Gitay has demonstrated, the self-conscious use of prose in a prophetic text, e.g., Isaiah 8, serves specific rhetorical interests (1991a:146–59). To argue that prophetic literature is essentially poetry is to ignore constitutive elements of prophetic behavior and literature attested in the Hebrew Bible (cf. the insightful discussion of Geller, 1983).[9]

Fourth, some claim to have identified a basic prophetic message, which allows one to think about a cohesive and coherent body of literature. Most typically, this message is identified as one involving ethical admonitions, especially, concerning justice and righteousness. A typical claim: "The basic teaching of the prophets is rather simple to understand, though difficult to carry out. As stated most clearly by Isaiah, it is 'Cease to do evil; learn to do good' (1:17)" (Steinberg:301). According to this model, the prophets function rather like teachers or preachers.

But this judgment, too, requires revision, for at least three reasons:

1) There is radical diversity of conviction on various topics by Israelite prophets, e.g., the place of Jerusalem in Isaiah (29:1–8) and Micah (3:12). And there is considerable variation on foci

---

[9] The respective roles of poetry and prose differ in prophetic books. For example, McKane has suggested that, in Jeremiah, "the poetry is a reservoir for the prose . . ." (269).

between literatures. In some, e.g., Hosea, veneration of Yahweh—and not Baʿal—is a primary topic; in others, e.g., Nahum, the existence and fate of a foreign nation is of sole importance.

2) Some kinds of prophetic literature do not present a "message," e.g., many of the narratives associated with Elisha. These legends are almost by definition amoral. Power rather than virtue is the *raison d'être* for these narratives. 2 Kgs 2:23–25 does not offer Elisha as a paragon of virtue but as a person filled with divine power. A similar judgment might be offered about the role of the prophet as diviner. The diviner may provide information sought by some individual, but there may be no larger "message."

3) Such a position does not take fully into account the revolutionary religious claims and demands of the prophets. It has been a recent commonplace to argue that the prophets were essentially conservative, calling Israel to follow norms that might be traced to pre-state Israel. Such norms were understood to be both religious/ritual and ethical. However, it is increasingly difficult to appeal to a particular ancient ethos with which the prophets stand in continuity. The more we know about the early veneration of Yahweh, the more heterodox that religion appears to have been (so, e.g., Smith, 1990). And the more one looks for a distinctively Israelite pre-state ethos, the more difficult it is to identify that with which the prophets might be standing in continuity (Lang, 1983).

4) Prophets disagreed; they could stand in conflict. The classic instances include the competition between Jeremiah and Hananiah (Jeremiah 28), Micaiah ben Imlah versus the prophets of Israel (1 Kings 22), and the man of God from Judah versus the old prophet from Bethel (1 Kings 13). These confrontations have often been described as instances of competition between true and false prophets. But this is to oversimplify the matter. So-called true prophets presented competing perspectives. Ezekiel and Zechariah offered conflicting visionary programs (Petersen, 1984). These two prophets provided different judgments about what a restored Israel might involve and how it might be achieved. Such competing prophetic perspectives make it difficult to contemplate a central prophetic message.

If one assesses critically these prejudgments, we are able to view prophetic literature in new ways. Prophetic literature, though not normally prosaic, was routinely composed in prose as well as poetry. Such diversity of literary style in some measure reflects the diverse roles of Israel's prophets. Prophets themselves, whether as speakers or writers, might compose prophetic literature. Nonetheless, prophets could act as prophets apart from this authorial role. Moreover, individuals other than intermediaries themselves could and did write prophetic literature. Given the diverse social and temporal contexts of prophetic activity, as well as the diverse forms of intermediation, it is difficult to distill an essential prophetic message from the prophetic literature.

III

In conclusion, I have argued that the notion of prophetic literature requires careful reconceptualization. A number of prejudgments have prevented us from recognizing fundamentally diverse forms of prophetic literature, diversity that reflects various forms of intermediation in ancient Israel. These fundamental forms include the divinatory chronicle, vision report, prophetic utterance, divine oracle, legend, and prophetic historiography. This claim should not be read as reductionism. Much of the literature associated with prophets is noteworthy, both as prose and as poetry. In addition, attention both to social dynamics and to literary features helps us avoid a view of the prophet as spirit-filled poet, ethical teacher, or preacher of repentance. The challenge for future comprehensive studies of prophetic literature will be that of enabling various critical perspectives to interact in mutually informative dialogue.

Works Consulted

Alter, R.

    1985   *The Art of Biblical Poetry*. New York: Basic Books.

Barton, J.

    1986   *Oracles of God: Perceptions of Ancient Prophecy in Israel after the Exile*. Oxford: Oxford University Press.

Berlin, A.

1989 "The Prophetic Literature of the Hebrew Bible." Pp. 114–19 in *Approaches to Teaching the Hebrew Bible as Literature in Translation*, ed. B. Olshen & Y. Feldman. New York: Modern Language Association of America.

Davis, E.

1989 *Swallowing the Scroll: Textuality and the Dynamics of Discourse in Ezekiel's Prophecy*. Bible and Literature Series 21. Sheffield: Almond Press.

Diamond, A. R.

1990 "Jeremiah's Confessions in the LXX and MT: A Witness to Developing Canonical Functions." *Vetus Testamentum* 40:33–50.

Dietrich, W.

1972 *Prophetie und Geschichte: Eine redaktionsgeschichtliche Untersuchung zum deuteronomistischen Gesschichtswerk*. Forschungen zur Religion und Literatur des Alten und Neuen Testaments, 108. Göttingen: Vandenhoeck & Ruprecht.

Freedman, D. N.

1977 "Pottery, Poetry, and Prophecy: An Essay on Biblical Poetry." *JBL* 96:5–26

1983 "Discourse on Prophetic Discourse." Pp. 141–58 in *The Quest for the Kingdom of God: Studies in Honor of George E. Mendenhall*, ed. H. Huffmon et al. Winona Lake: Eisenbrauns.

Geller, S.

1983 "Were the Prophets Poets?" *Prooftexts* 3:211–21.

Gitay, Y.

1989 "Oratorical Rhetoric: The Question of Prophetic Language with Special Attention to Isaiah." *Amsterdamse Cahiers* 10:72–83.

1991a   *Isaiah and his Audience: The Structure and Meaning of Isaiah 1–12.* Studia Semitica Neerlandica, 30. Assen: Van Gorcum.

1991b   "Rhetorical Criticism and the Prophetic Discourse." Pp. 13–24 in *Persuasive Artistry: Studies in New Testament Rhetoric in Honor of George A. Kennedy.* JSNTSup 50. Sheffield: Sheffield Academic Press.

Heschel, A.

1962   "Prophecy and Poetic Inspiration." Pp. 147–69 in *The Prophets, Vol 2.* New York: Harper and Row.

Horst, F.

1960   "Die Visionsschilderungen der alttestamentlichen Propheten." *EvT* 20:193–205.

Huffmon, H.

1992   "Ancient Near Eastern Prophecy." Pp. 447–82 in *The Anchor Bible Dictionary,* vol. 5. New York: Doubleday.

Jeffrey, D.

1990   "How to Read the Hebrew Prophets." *Bucknell Review* 33/2:282–98.

Jeremias, C.

1977   *Die Nachtgesichte des Sacharja: Untersuchungen zu ihrer Stellung im Zusammenhang der Visionsberichte im Alten Testament und zu ihrem Bildmaterial.* FRLANT 117. Göttingen: Vandenhoeck & Ruprecht.

Lang, B.

1983   *Monotheism and the Prophetic Minority: An Essay in Biblical History and Sociology.* The Social World of Biblical Antiquity Series, 1. Sheffield: Almond Press.

Lowth, R.

1983   *Lectures on the Sacred Poetry of the Hebrews.* London: T. Begg. (1753, *De Sacra Poesi Hebraeorum*)

March, W. E.

1974　　"Prophecy." Pp. 141–77 in *Old Testament Form Criticism*, ed. John H. Hayes. Trinity University Monograph Series in Religion, 2. San Antonio: Trinity University Press.

McKane, W.

1984　　"Relations Between Poetry and Prose in the Book of Jeremiah with Special Reference to Jeremiah iii 6–11 and xi 14–17." Pp. 269–84 in *A Report to the Nations*, ed. L. Perdue & B. Kovacs. Winona Lake: Eisenbrauns.

Moore, M.

1990a　　*The Balaam Traditions: Their Character and Development.* SBLDS 113. Atlanta: Scholars Press.

1990b　　"Another Look at Balaam." *Revue Biblique* 97:359–78.

Overholt, T.

1989　　*Channels of Prophecy: The Social Dynamics of Prophetic Activity.* Minneapolis: Fortress.

Petersen, D.

1981　　*The Roles of Israel's Prophets.* JSOTSup 17. Sheffield: University of Sheffield.

1984　　"Zechariah's Visions: A Theological Perspective." *Vetus Testamentum* 34:195–206.

Rofé, A.

1988　　*The Prophetical Stories: The Narratives about the Prophets in the Hebrew Bible. Their Literary Types and History.* Publications of the Perry Foundation for Biblical Research in the Hebrew University. Jerusalem: Magnes.

Sister, M.

1934　　"Die Typen der prophetischen Visionen in der Bibel." *Monatsschrift für Geschichte und Wissenschaft des Judentums* 77:393–430.

Smith, M.
1990 *The Early History of God: Yahweh and the Other Deities in Ancient Israel*. San Francisco: Harper and Row.

Starr, I.
1990 *Queries to the Sungod: Divination and Politics in Sargonid Assyria*. State Archives of Assyria, IV; Helsinki: Helsinki University Press.

Steinberg, T.
1990 "Isaiah the Poet." *Bucknell Review* 33/2:299–310.

Sweeney, M.
1988 *Isaiah 1–4 and the Post-Exilic Understanding of the Isaianic Tradition*. BZAW 171. Berlin: Walter de Gruyter.

Tucker, G. M.
1978 "Prophetic Speech." *Interpretation* 32:31–45.
1987 "The Role of the Prophets and the Role of the Church." Pp. 159–74 in *Prophecy in Israel: Search for an Identity*, ed. D. Petersen. Issues in Religion and Theology, 10. Philadelphia: Fortress.

Utzschneider, H.
1989 *Künder oder Schreiber? Eine These zum Problem der "Schriftprophetie" auf Grund von Maleachi 1,6–2,9*. Beiträge zur Erforschung des Alten Testaments und des antiken Judentum 19. Frankfurt: Peter Lang.

Vermeylen, J.
1977–78 *Du prophète Isaïe à l'apocalyptique. Isaïe, I–XXXV, miroir d'un demi-millénaire d'expérience religieuse en Israél*, 2 vols. Ebib. Paris: J. Gabalda.

Westermann, C.
1967 *Basic Forms of Prophetic Speech*. Philadelphia: Fortress.

Wiklander, B.

    1984   *Prophecy as Literature: A Text-Linguistic and Rhetorical Approach to Isaiah 2–4*. ConBOT 22. Lund: Gleerup.

Williamson, H. G. M.

    1994   *The Book called Isaiah: Deutero-Isaiah's Role in Composition and Redaction*. Oxford: Clarendon.

Wilson, R.

    1980   *Prophecy and Society in Ancient Israel*. Philadelphia: Fortress.

THE PROJECTION OF THE PROPHET:
A RHETORICAL PRESENTATION
OF THE PROPHET JEREMIAH
(ACCORDING TO JER 1:1–19)

Yehoshua Gitay

The prophetic books have inspired their readers for generations. Recent scholarship regarding the readers' perception focuses on the prophetic books as a whole, viz., it traces the literary and thematic structure of the entire body of books.[1] The growing interest in the books and their literary shape discouraged the scholarly concern about the figure of the individual prophet (Ward; Carroll, 55–64). However, readers of prophetic literature associate the books with their ascribed prophetic authors: the two seem inseparable. So whether the books still preserve an historical prophetic figure (Barstad), or should be considered as a unhistorical "presentation of the prophet" (Ackroyd), the prophetic books reflect the struggle of individuals. That is, prophets who are inspired by God's revelation to deliver a message which rebukes their audience. Given the harsh tone of the prophetic speeches, the books represent the prophets as provoking antipathy. As the prophet is aware of his audience's probable reaction to his critical message, the prophetic books reflect the inner tensions of the prophets as sensitive human beings, and their rhetorical attempts to reach their antagonistic audiences. Remember the attempt to execute Micah following his speech against the Temple (reported in Jer 26:18–19), Jeremiah imprisoned (Jer 37:12–16), Amos's re-enforced exile to Judah (Amos 7:10–15), and Isaiah's withdrawal into silence after the negative response to his speeches (Isa 8:16–

---

[1] For a survey of current research on the book of Isaiah, which is reflective of contemporary studies of the prophetic literature in general, see Williamson, 1–18 and the bibliography cited therein. Also see Carroll, 33–86.

18). The literary reports of the clashes between the prophets, who take personal risks in order to deliver their message, and their immediate audiences are not sufficiently addressed in contemporary research.

The aim of this paper is to attempt to address this imbalance. I intend to provide a rhetorical presentation of a singular prophet, Jeremiah, focusing on his prophetic mission. This study does not however engage the question of whether the literary depiction of Jeremiah in chapter 1 is historical or a reflection of a later prophetic presentation. My present concern is about whether Jeremiah has been presented in a manner that responds to his immediate historical audience or to the readers of the scribe(s) who shaped the book. Either way, the author did not create an "impersonal man in general," but a lively individual who might be an implied version of the author her/himself (Booth, 70–71).

The beginning of the book indicates the role of its prophet: "The words of Jeremiah son of Hilkiah . . ." (Jer 1:1). The utterance at the introduction of the book, Jeremiah's call, is the prophet's initiation into his office. The call of the prophet is apparently a dramatic moment in his life, and one could expect a vivid description of Jeremiah's call in the book ascribed to him. However, the narrative uses a stereotyped stylistic structure (Habel); and one should question whether this formulaic approach concealed any expression of personal feeling that might reflect the prophet's intimate religious experience.

The act of publishing contradicts the intimate tone of a private affair; it indicates that the narrator seeks to turn the personal affair of Jeremiah's call into a public event. Indeed, a number of clashes that take place between Jeremiah and his opponents revolve around the question of prophetic authenticity. Jeremiah's frustrating confrontation with Hananiah, son of Azur (chap. 28), exemplifies the confusion. The narrative repeatedly refers to Hananiah as a prophet (vv. 1, 5, 10, 12, 15, 17), while Jeremiah is also called a prophet (vv. 5, 6, 10, 11, 12). Thus, the literary account purposely makes it difficult for the reader to distinguish between the two figures. Both claim to deliver God's authentic message. Furthermore, Jeremiah's recorded tensions with the authorities, outlined in chapter 26, point out the need to prove to the officials that he was the genuine prophet:

> Then the priests and the prophets said to the officials and to all the people. This man deserves the sentence of death because he has prophesied against this city . . . Then Jeremiah spoke to the officials and all the people, saying: It is the Lord who sent me to prophesy against this house and this city all the words you have heard . . . for in truth the Lord sent me to you to speak all these words in your ears. (26:10–15)

Jeremiah is confronted with other situations that question his prophetic office. Thus, it becomes necessary to establish an atmosphere of trust in him as the authorized prophet since the issue at stake is that of prophetic authority. Hence, the traditional form of the prophetic call is functional: it presents Jeremiah's commission to prophetic office as the sacred "myth" of God's elected messengers (Frye, 31–52). Thus, the prologue of the book is designed to perpetuate in writing, through a literary form that signifies a traditional prophetic call, the monumental act of appointing Jeremiah to the prophetic office (Carroll, 94).

A form critical analysis of the genre of Jeremiah's call reveals close similarities to the narrative of Moses' call (Ex 3:1–4:17; JE and 6:2–13, 28; 7:1–5; P), as well as to Gideon's commission (Judg 6:11–17). In each case the appointee first refuses to take the office, ascribing his hesitation to a handicap of speech (Moses) or to the weak oratory of inexperienced youth (Gideon, Jeremiah). Consequently, God provides signs, ensuring the success of the appointee, who eventually accepts the commission (Holladay, 27–28). The form of the genre plays a critical role in identifying its intention; and the presentation of Jeremiah's call in the formulaic form of the initiation of outstanding biblical leaders makes its point.

However, the form in itself does not determine the force of the utterance. For example, in a love poem it is not only the form that transmits the force of the feelings. An utterance must act, and it must create an event in order to be forceful. Speech-act theory (introduced by J. L. Austin) holds that many human utterances do something, perform an act, and that in such utterances we can identify a basic *illocutionary* force: in saying x, a speaker does y. Thus, the utterance may represent a tension between singularity and collectivity; the canonized form against the *illocutionary* force. This dialectical relationship between the diachronic reading of Jeremiah's call, on the one hand, and the *illocutionary* force of the speech, on the other, is the core of the art of an effective reading of the text (Cohen, 171–205).

The dialogue characterizes the genre of the call. God approaches the appointee who first refuses, then God responds. Moses refuses straightforwardly: "Who am I that I should go to Pharaoh, and bring the Israelites out of Egypt?" (Ex 3:11), or: ". . . since I am a poor speaker, why should Pharaoh listen to me?" (Ex 6:29–30).

Similarly God says to Gideon: "I hereby commission you" (Judg 6:14); and the response is: "But sir, how can I deliver Israel? My clan is the weakest . . ." (v. 15). Both Moses and Gideon are commissioned, and both of them refuse explicitly, employing an expected form of refusal. However, Jeremiah does not refuse God's commission directly; he just says: "Ah, Lord God! Truly I do not know how to speak" (v. 6). An act has been performed; Jeremiah complains that he does not know how to speak, and God understands that Jeremiah means something else—that he is refusing to accept the prophetic office. This dynamic confrontation between God and Jeremiah performs a speech-act that is not perceivable through the diachronic form. That is, the dialogue itself does not create a duel confrontation; the speech situation creates the action, presenting a forceful utterance: Jeremiah says x and he does y. Consequently, the readers cannot let the expected formula guide their reading; the act of reading must respond to the speech-act situation.

Furthermore, a close analysis of the style of the dialogue that takes place between God and Jeremiah reveals a deliberate attempt to present the call as a vivid and unconventional utterance. God approaches Jeremiah in verse: lines a plus b of v. 5 form a symmetric parallel in harmonic meter: 4:4. A characteristic word-pair is noticeable as well: רחם/בטן. The structure of the verse is rhythmical, symmetrical and aural. Attention should be paid to the unusual repetition בטרם, which appears at the beginning of the first two lines, as well as to the pun אצורך and the alliteration תצא and the assonance ך. However, the third line (c) stands alone without a parallel, and the prosodic parallel pattern has been broken.

The question is how style works. The formalist Havranek made a distinction between two types of styles: automatization versus foregrounding:

> By automatization we mean such a use of the devices of language, in isolation or in combination with each other, as is useful for a certain expressive purpose, that is, such a use that the expression itself does not attract any attention . . . By foregrounding, on the other hand, we mean the use of the devices of the language in such a way that this use itself attracts attention and is perceived as uncommon, as deprived of automization, as deautomatized . . . (Carter and Nash, 4).

The last unparalleled line (v. 5c) is perceived as uncommon, and is therefore designed to attract attention. Furthermore, the syntactical and semantic structure of lines a+b is very similar: each line starts with the same word, followed by a verb that is linked to another through a strong sound relationship(צ). However, v. 5c is again exceptional: the repeated בטרם disappears; a noun starts the line, and a new structure has been introduced, breaking the routine. Thus, the audience's attention has been attracted to the height of the entire verse: "I appoint you a prophet to the nations." Nevertheless, a total break of the entire structure may also distract the audience. And some link with the "automatization" must be preserved, otherwise the established code of communication would be affected. Indeed, the last word of v. 5c נתתיך, is linked with the ends of the two previous lines (הקדשתיך, ידעתיך) through their common sound.

In contrast to the vivid symmetrical and rhythmical poetic structure of v. 5 that conveys God's speech to Jeremiah in order to appoint him as a prophet, v. 6, which proclaims Jeremiah's response, is structured un-poetically and un-rhythmical:

ואמר אהה אדני ה׳ הנה לא־ידעתי דבר כי נער אנכי:

> Then I said: Ah, Lord God! Truly I do not know how to speak, for I am only a boy.

The difference in style reflects two mental situations that characterize the utterance: the Commander who harmonically stylizes His call of appointment versus the confused subject whose words are unable to reach the level of God's sublime proclamation. The unparalleled structure of Jeremiah's response re-enforces the focus on each word. However, a conventional stylistic response to such a dramatic situation might be perceived as dull and ineffective. The word אהה, which opens Jeremiah's response, connotes a stressful condition that motivates his desperate appeal to God. (compare: Josh 7:7, Judg 6:22, 11:35, Jer 4:10, 14:31, 32:17, and more). Indeed, this stylistic expression conveys a feeling of despair and panic, which successfully reflects sincere feeling. Furthermore, we recall our earlier observation of the speech force of Jeremiah's response, and now we are able to conclude that both v. 5 and v. 6—God's appointment of Jeremiah to be a prophet and Jeremiah's response—are designed to attract attention to the main points. The verses also are stylized in a form that is designed to reflect the excitement of the moment, seeking to affect genuine feelings.

The public presentation of the call projects an additional rhetorical goal. Various prophets, while addressing a message of doom, find it necessary to emphasize that they deliver the judgment not because they wish to, but because they have no other choice; they are compelled to deliver God's punishment. Amos explains his message of destruction thus:

> The lion has roared;
> who will not fear?
> The Lord God has spoken;
> who can but not prophesy? (3:8)

The prophet feels that he needs to protect his image in front of his audience; he is not his people's adversary but he must deliver God's word (For further discussion see, Gitay, 1980a).

Rhetoric, the art of effective presentation, sheds light on the function of the apologetic tone of the prophetic speech. The speakers clearly must win their audience's trust, otherwise they will lose their confidence. The speakers who are unable to gain their audience's trust will fail to influence them. Aristotle describes the problem thus:

> But since rhetoric exists to effect the giving decisions—the hearers decide between one political speaker and another . . . the orator must not only try to make the judgment of his speech demonstrative and worthy of belief; he must also make his own character look right and put his hearers, who are to decide, into the right frame of mind . . . it adds much to an orator's influence that his own character should look right . . . (Rhetoric, 1377b)

In this way Amos seeks his audience's understanding in order to achieve his rhetorical goal: to appeal to his audience. Similarly, Jeremiah is presented as one of the people, and not as their deliberate opponent. It is not his idea to convey God's message of judgment; he has no freedom of choice since, as we are told, he was appointed even before his birth (v. 5). The divine commission of individuals or nations before their birth is a biblical convention that is not used very often. (For Egyptian parallels see Beyerlin, 28–30).

For instance, Samson "shall be a nazirite to God from birth. It is he who shall begin to deliver Israel from the hand of the Philistines" (Judg 13:5–6). And the redemption of Israel is ensured since her formation: "Thus says the Lord who made you, who formed you in the womb and will help you . . ." (Isa 44:2; also see Isa 44:24, 49:1, 5 and Hos 9:11; 12:4, as well as Gen 25:23). The reference to the בטן ("belly") connotes not the physicality of the formation. The belly is the place of emotions, thus, conveying the intimate relationship between God and the chosen one. The intention is to stir the audience's sympathy and confidence in the chosen one. (Carroll, 97–98). Jer 1:5 functions therefore as the prophet's ethical appeal (consult further Gitay, 1983, 1991). His unique portrayal as God's messenger seeks to refute any opposition. Furthermore, the emphasis on the intimacy between God and Jeremiah seeks to proclaim that his personality should not cause antagonism (as the Book alludes repeatedly: see, for instance, 11:21, 15:10, 20:7–10) because initially he rejected the prophetic appointment; he is reluctantly God's closest representative.

The conclusion that the utterance seeks to establish Jeremiah's credibility also explains the frequency of the employment of the combination ויהי דבר ה' אלי or ויאמר ה' אלי in chapter 1 (vv. 4, 7, 9, 11, 12, 13, 14). These combinations in direct speech אלי ("to me") are employed seven times in the utterance, stressing the sacred connotation of the direct communication by the Divine with His prophet. The combination ויאמר ה' אלי is specifically utilized in order to emphasize that the communication is authentic. Thus insists Balaam: . . . I will bring back word to you, just as the Lord speaks to me" (כאשר ידבר ה' אלי Num 22:8), or: "But Micaiah said: As the Lord lives, whatever the Lord says to me, that I will speak" (1 Kgs 22:14). The speakers in both instances make the point distinctly through the employment of the phrase, דבר ה' אלי, that they convey the authentic words without having any other choice. The prophetic authority has been established through the stress on direct communication between God and the prophet without an intermediary.

The meaning of v. 9:

> Then the Lord put out his hand and touched my mouth; and the Lord said to me, 'now I have put my words in your mouth.'

הנה נתתי דברי בפיך.

is elucidated in 36:17–18, in which Baruch is asked specifically about the authority of his reading of the scroll; his answer is that Jeremiah would dictate to him and he would write. "He dictates all these words to me", translates the New Revised Standard Version. However, the Massoretic text is more precise: מפיו יקרא אלי ("from his mouth he directs me"). The authority has been established—from mouth to ears.

We have already noticed that the stereotyped structure of the call does not suppress the personal portrayal of Jeremiah. The question whether the narrative of the call reflects the prophetic experience and if so, how it does it, is indeed important in considering the rhetorical impact.

Jeremiah's response in v. 6 invites a comparison to another sort of "Man of God", the shaman. According to M. Eliade (79–80), the initiation of the shaman involves ecstatic behavior, unconscious reflections and a state of trance. Indeed, Jeremiah's verbal reflection on his appointment mirrors some excitement אהה but the response is coherent; and his hesitation to accept the mission is reasonably motivated. Rhetorically, this logical structure is noticeable because the personal initiation is orientated to the public, presenting Jeremiah's ethos in a manner suited to the audience.

Furthermore, the call of the mission is proclaimed through a linguistic-visual medium that carries its own appeal. This is the exclusive language of religious experience, which seeks in our case to convey the experience in a coherent language. Thus, R. Otto called for a distinction between "a belief in the reality beyond the senses and to have experience of it also" (Otto, 143). He continues:

> Genuine divination, has nothing whatever to do with natural law . . . It is not concerned at all with the way in which a phenomenon—be it event, person or thing—came into existence, but with what it means, that is, with its significance as a "sign" of the holy. (145)

There is a difference between "what we see" and "what does it mean." Jeremiah's utterance shares with the audience Jeremiah's religious experience in its dual meanings—the explicit or the external, and the implicit or the internal. God demonstrates to Jeremiah that He is consistent (a situation which made Jonah fearful).[2] The demonstration is based on observation and deduction. In v. 11 Jeremiah is asked: "what do you see?": מה אתה ראה? At first glance this is a simple question, employed in order to develop some sort of a dialogue as is the case in a similar literary context: Amos's vision of the כלוב קיץ a basket of summer fruit (Amos 8:1–2) in which he is asked "what do you see"? He answers and God explains. That is, Amos does not enjoy the

---

[2] Jonah demanded consistency; the people of *Nineveh* committed a sin and they should be punished. However, Jonah's situation differs from Jeremiah's. See my recent study (Gitay: 1995).

freedom of defining the objective of his observation; the question
is merely a vehicle for promoting God's statement. However,
Jeremiah is asked to define his observation, and God praises him
for this: היטבת לראות, "you have seen well." Therefore, we may
conclude that Jeremiah had freedom of choice, that he could
point to other objects or describe the phenomenon differently,
rather than define the object as מקל שקד. However, his insights
led him correctly. The commendation "you have seen well" is
designed to reassure hesitant members of the audience who doubt
Jeremiah's prophetic credibility.

The utterance motivates a comparison between Jeremiah's
appropriate definition and his earlier hesitation to fulfill the
prophetic office. Making the right choice, Jeremiah is depicted as
an intelligent man with insight. Nevertheless, there is a need to
provide the internal meaning of the vision, revealed only by God.
The branch of an almond tree, the שקד, has an implicit meaning;
God's consistency, ש(ו)קד. Explicitly, the שקד is blossoming in
the early winter. Implicitly, however, this annual cycle of nature
conveys an internal religious meaning; nature does not exist in
itself but is due to God's consistency. The utterance depicts
Jeremiah as sharing with his audience his religious experience. By
doing so, the audience is taken into the prophetic intimate world
of Jeremiah. Jeremiah is not characterized any more as an ordinary
human being, but conveys through his experience the internal
meaning, that is, the sign of the Holy. In short, the public
presentation of the implicit meaning of the sign demonstrates the
religious validity of Jeremiah's message. That is, natural
phenomena perceived by ordinary human beings as simple natural
events are no longer regarded as external conventions, but carry
an internal religious dimension. The latter conveys God's intention
in the prophetic speech. Rhetorically, this is an appeal through the
religious mystery, which converts the conventional natural
observation into a profound religious manifestation. The prophet
Jeremiah is presented as possessing a secret knowledge; a clear
message has been conveyed to the audience: Jeremiah's prophecy
is God's truthful manifestation.

The utterance encourages Jeremiah to be strong, and to deliver God's message without fear (v. 8). The promise is proclaimed by literary means, strengthened by the use of figuration in v. 18:

> And I for my part have made you today a fortified city, an iron pillar, and a bronze wall, against the whole land against the kings of Judah, its princes, its priests, and the people of the land.

The first question to be discussed is the function of the figure in the realm of persuasive discourse. God's endurance in v. 8—"Do not be afraid of them, for I am with you to deliver you, says the Lord"—is not a mathematical proof for the already perplexed Jeremiah. Instead, the statement conveys a feeling, or seeks to establish a state of mind, which might not be self-evident for the hesitant. In short, the sort of statement that conveys matters of opinion requires proof. The scientific proof in matters of attitude, feelings or opinions is replaced by the method of quasi-proof, presented through the employment of figurative language. The metaphor is a persuasive means that seeks to present reality. The audience perceives the depicted reality as an un-refutable element, which replaces in the course of the discourse the comparable matter that is subjected to unscientific methods of argumentation (Perelman, 53–80). That is, the argumentative process takes place between the familiar and un-refutable reality, now the metaphor, and the audience's perception: fortified city, iron pillar, and a bronze wall; this is now the un-refutable reality. Hence, the metaphor is an integral part of the argumentation of the language of the call (contra Holladay, 24–25, who failed to read the utterance as a rhetorical-argumentative presentation).

Attention should be given to the stylistic presentation of v. 18: עמוד ברזל. These words are omitted in the LXX, perhaps, because of the uniqueness of the combination. However, the Massoretic verse presents a parallel to the iron pillar: חמות נחשת. The word-pair: נחשת/ברזל is common (see Lev 26:19, Deut 8:9, 28:23, Psa 150:16, and more). Thus, v. 18 is not too unfamiliar; the unfamiliar phrase is tied together to the paralleled line on the basis of an established literary convention. The value of the unfamiliar combination is that the metaphor does not become a cliché, but arouses the curiosity of the audience which, given their oral culture which is based on conventions of speech, is quick to identify the unique linguistic use (See further Gitay, 1980b). However, there is a communicative danger: the audience may lose the code of communication that is essential for perceiving the text. In order to avoid this problem the entire linguistic formulation of v. 18 is dressed in a familiar communicative code. The linguistic structure shows great sensitivity to the impact of the address.

This rhetorical presentation leads to the conclusion that in terms of theme, the call and the assurances to the prophet both through the vision and the metaphor create, on the basis of the flow of thought, a unified rhetorical discourse (For further discussion consult, Gitay, 1983).

In summary, Jeremiah chapter 1 is an utterance that presents the impact of God's initiation of Jeremiah as a prophet. The utterance seeks to prove Jeremiah's prophetic authority in response to challenges to the validity of his prophetic message. The stress on Jeremiah's prophetic authority and the authenticity of his message paves the road for accepting Jeremiah as a true prophet and deliverer of God's message. It is important to perpetuate in writing the personal dimension of Jeremiah's commission and the implication of his personal hesitation. Jeremiah's personal struggle and the pressure to deliver the message is the core of his prophetic endeavor, which is the center of his literary presentation. The personal factor in the context of the prophetic book is, therefore, a crucial element that must take its place in current scholarship, whether through the diachronic historical approach or by the means of the synchronic school that searches for the meaning of the book as a whole.

Jeremiah 1 delivers a prophetic message that also paints colorful images of a person who is commissioned as a prophet. The message to the audience or reader is obvious since the lively portrayal of the prophetic figure is not accidental. The book cannot stand by itself without a figure. The speeches are not merely an oration of sermons or an anthology of laws, as one might, for example, consider the literary essence of the book of

Deuteronomy. Rather the book of Jeremiah is based on the personal struggle of a prophet in his effort to deliver an unpleasant message. And the beginning, chapter 1, points out that the prophetic figure and the book ascribed to him are inseparable.

Works Consulted

Ackroyd, P. R.

1978   "Isaiah 1–12: Presentation of a Prophet." Pp. 16–48 in *Congress Volume: Göttingen 1977. SVT* 29. Leiden: Brill.

Austin, J. L.

1962   *How to Do Things with Words.* Cambridge: Harvard University.

Barstad, H. M.

1993   "No Prophets? Recent Development in Biblical Prophetic Research and the Ancient Eastern Prophecy." *JSOT* 57:39–60.

Beyerlin, W. (ed.)

1978   *Near Eastern Religious Texts Relating to the Old Testament.* Philadelphia: Westminster.

Booth, W. C.

1961   *The Rhetoric of Fiction.* Chicago: University of Chicago Press.

Carroll, R. P.

1986   *Jeremiah.* Philadelphia: Westminster.

Carter, R. and W. Nash

1990   *Seeing Through Language.* Oxford: Blackwell.

Cohen, R.

1994   "Speech-Acts and *Sprachspiele*." Pp.171–205 in *Modern Critical Theory and Classical Literature,* ed. I. De Jong and J. P. Sullivan. Leiden: Brill.

Eliade, M.

1960   *Myth, Dreams, and Mysteries.* New York: Harper & Row.

Frye, N.

1982   *The Great Code.* San Diego: Harvest.

Gitay, Y.

1980a   "A Study of Amos's Art of Speech: A Rhetorical Analysis
          of Amos 3:1–15." *CBQ* 42:293–309.

1980b   "Deutero Isaiah — Oral or Written?" *JBL* 99:185–97.

1981   *Prophecy and Persuasion.* Bonn: Linguistica Biblica.

1983   "Reflections on the Study of the Prophetic Discourse."
          VT 33:207–21.

1991   *Isaiah and His Audience.* Assen: Van Gorcum.

1995   The Prophecy of Anti-Rhetoric." Pp. 211–21 in
          *Fortunate the Eyes That See: Essays in Honor of David Noel
          Freedman,* ed. A. B. Beck et al. Grand Rapids:
          Eerdmans.

Habel, N. C.

1963   "The Form and the Significance of the Call Narratives."
          ZAW 77:297–323.

Holladay, W. L.

1988   *Jeremiah 1.* Philadelphia: Westminster.

Nash, W. See R. Carter.

Otto, R.

1923   *The Idea of the Holy.* London: Oxford University Press.

Perelman, Ch.

1982   *The Realm of Rhetoric.* Notre Dame: University of Notre
          Dame Press.

Ward, J. M.

1988   "The Eclipse of the Prophet in Contemporary
          Prophetic Studies," *USQR* 42:97–104.

Williamson, H. G. M.
   1994   *The Book Called Isaiah.* Oxford: Clarendon.

BETWEEN GOD AND MAN:
PROPHETS IN ANCIENT ISRAEL[*]

David Noel Freedman

Prophets in the Bible claim to be both foretellers and forthtellers, and base their claims upon their personal and private access to Yahweh, the God of Israel and ruler of history—past, present, and future. In important ways, they share claims and professional status with prophetic counterparts in other cultures, mainly diviners of different kinds, who also predicted future events and claimed individual access to the realm of the divine.[1] A striking example of such cross-cultural interaction is found in the person and experience of Balaam, the Aramean diviner who acquires

---

[*] I would like to thank John Huddlestun (formerly Arthur F. Thurnau Fellow at the University of Michigan) for his assistance with this article. John edited, revised, and in some cases expanded my original text, and also added the endnotes and bibliography. However, I assume final responsibility for the article's contents.

[1] On prophecy/divination in the ancient Near East (excluding Israel), see Lanczkowski 1960; Černý 1962:35–48; Nougayrol 1966; Leclant 1968; Nougayrol 1968; Ramot 1972:812–909; Wilson 1980:89–134; Loewe and Blacker 1981:142–90; Weippert 1981, and his essay in Weippert, Seybold, and Weippert 1985:55–93; Ellis 1989; and, most recently, Huffmon 1992; for Egypt, note also the relevant entries *Orakel, Prophetie,* and *Verkünden* in *Lexikon der Ägyptologie,* eds. W. Helck, E. Otto, and W. Westendorf. 7 Vols. (Wiesbaden: Harrassowitz, 1975–92).

Of particular importance for the evaluation of prophecy in ancient Israel are the texts unearthed from the middle Euphrates site known as Mari (Tell Ḥariri); for orientation and further bibliography, see generally the articles of Margueron (archaeology), Durand (texts), and Keck (bibliography) in volume 4 of the *Anchor Bible Dictionary* (New York: Doubleday, 1992), pp. 525–38. For Mari's relevance to prophecy in the Hebrew Bible, see Ellermeier 1968; Huffmon 1968 and 1992; Moran 1969; Noort 1977; Malamat 1980, 1987, and 1989; and Schmitt 1982. Note also the various articles in the *Biblical Archaeologist* for June 1984 (Vol. 47, no. 2).

Of more general interest is the comparative study of biblical and ancient Near Eastern prophetic motifs by Weinfeld (1977).

prophetic status and function in the service (unexpected and unenthusiastic) of Yahweh the God of Israel (Num 22–24).[2] While there is a radical and dramatic switchover from one patron or client to another, and from cursing to blessing Israel under irresistible pressure from Israel's God, Balaam's role, status, and activity remain much the same. The categories and patterns of prophetic behavior that emerge from within the Balaam and ancient Near Eastern traditions are largely the same. As in other related matters, e.g., worship, sacrifice, and ethical principles or practices, Israel shared much with its neighbors and, in many respects, was a late-comer and borrower in relation to the great civilizations and high cultures of Mesopotamia and Egypt.

Nevertheless, granting their common cultural heritage, one cannot overlook the fact that, *in its fully developed character*, the phenomenon of biblical prophecy stands apart in many respects from other religions of the ancient Near East. Indeed, with few exceptions, the surviving materials of pagan antiquity retain only academic interest, whereas the prophetic texts of the Hebrew Bible continue to speak across the centuries with words that have direct bearing on our lives and meaning for our civilization. More often than not, and specifically in matters of religion, the people of the Bible formed and forged something distinctive and different from all that came before or was contemporaneous with them. This is especially the case with prophecy, at least as we find it presented in the Hebrew Bible.

We shall approach our vast subject by highlighting some of the more important elements or components of biblical prophecy, including the prophet's call, the vexing question of false prophecy, the ethics of prophetic religion, and the prophet's role as intercessor.

---

[2] Extra-biblical evidence for the existence of Balaam has come forth in a rare manner through the discovery of plaster texts from the Transjordanian site of Deir ʿAlla, which recount the experience of a seer of the gods (*ḥzh ʾlhn*) named Balaam son of Beor (*blʿm br bʿr*). See Hoftizer and van der Kooij 1976 and 1991; Rofé 1979 (Appendix); Kaufman 1980; Hackett 1980; Levine 1985; Lemaire 1985; Puech 1985; and Layton 1992.

The Prophet's Experience of God

The prophetic movement as an actual historic phenomenon—and an essential part of Israel's theo-political structure—had its beginnings with Samuel and his followers in the 11th c. BCE at the point of transition from the era of the judges to the beginnings of the monarchy and the installation of Saul as royal head of the Israelite Confederation (e.g., 1 Sam 3:19–21; 9–10). Prophets, beginning with Samuel, played a significant, if not decisive, role in establishing and also in censoring the monarchy (e.g., 1 Sam 10–13; 15; 16:1–13).[3] They remained an integral part of Israelite society as long as the monarchy survived—and even beyond, while there was still thought or hope of restoring the kingship of the House of David.

For biblical writers, the factors and features of prophecy were seen in earlier heroes of faith and role models in Israel's experience; therefore, the patriarchs generally, and Abraham in particular, could be called prophets (e.g., Gen 20:7, where it is the intercessory power and privilege of the patriarch that are described as prophetic). More emphatically, Moses is regarded and treated as the prophet *par excellence* and *non pareil* because, of all the leaders of Israel, he attained the highest level of intimacy with the deity, and fulfilled most completely the role and responsibility of a prophet.[4] He is set apart by the biblical writers/editors as unique among the prophets, the standard and gauge by which all others are to be measured. The ultimate point of difference—one of quality more than degree—is that, while God spoke to prophets generally through visions, auditions, or dreams, with Moses he spoke face to face (Deut 34:10–12) or mouth to mouth (Exod

---

[3] For the period as a whole and the role of Samuel in it, see generally, Albright 1961; Boecker 1969; Richter 1970:13–56; Birch 1976; Mettinger 1976:64–98; Mayes 1977; Veijola 1977:30–99; Crüsemann 1978:54–84; Wilson 1978 and 1980:166–84; Blenkinsopp 1983:61–68; Evans 1983; and Miller and Hayes 1986:120–48.

[4] For the figure of Moses in general, see, e.g., Gressmann 1913; Meeks 1967; Schmid 1968; Childs 1974; Weimar 1980; Coats 1988; and Fischer 1989. On Moses as prophet, see (in addition to the relevant sections of the above) Muilenburg 1965; Perlitt 1971; Wilson 1980:156–66; and Renaud 1986.

33:11). Whereas other prophets only sense the presence of the deity, Moses sees his actual form and person (Num 12:8; cf. Exod 33:9, 17–23 and 34:5–8).

On the basis of the biblical accounts of the prophets and their experiences, we can piece together the components to make up a suitable prophetic profile.

(1) *The Call*. The divine call and commission mark the beginning of the prophet's career.[5] For many of the prophets, the circumstances and some details are given; whereas for others, the specific data are lacking, but we may suppose or assume some similar experience. In all recorded cases, the details are striking and distinctive: no two are exactly the same, although they share important elements.[6] We possess sufficient data to fill out a composite picture for people like Moses (Exod 3:1–12), Samuel (1 Sam 3:1–14), and Elisha (1 Kgs 19:19–21), along with the great literary prophets such as Amos (Amos 7:14–15), Hosea (Hos 1:2–11), Isaiah (Isa 6), Jeremiah (Jer 1:4–10), and Ezekiel (Ezek 1:1—3:15). Yet we lack information about the call of prophets such as Nathan, Ahijah, and Elijah, to mention only a few. The call is initiated by God and is often accompanied by a vision(s), along with some unusual or miraculous occurrence (e.g., Moses and the burning bush). It is the combination of circumstances that persuades the prophet that he is not hallucinating, but is in direct contact with the living God.

(2) *The Commission*. The call is always accompanied by a commission. The purpose is to enlist or draft the prophet to carry out a mission or duty, in other words, to do something in response to the call. He is supposed to respond positively, or at least acquiesce in his role as messenger/agent of the deity. Some are very reluctant to take on such responsibility and thus make excuses

---

5 On call narratives generally, see Lindblom 1962:182–97; Habel 1965; von Rad 1965:50–69; Baltzer 1968; Henry 1969:11–41; Richter 1970; Long 1972 and 1977; Zimmerli 1979:97–100; and Buss 1982.

6 For those common elements and motifs, see, for example, Habel 1965, who isolates the following: divine confrontation, introductory word, commission, objection, reassurance, and sign.

or attempt other means to evade their calling. Examples of such are Moses, Jeremiah, and, above all, Jonah (although in the latter case, the story seems to refer to a later commission as opposed to an initial call or contact with God).[7] Others, for example, Isaiah, Ezekiel, and perhaps Hosea, are eager to carry out their task and hasten to do so. The basic rules for the prophet, the "marching orders" as it were, are given succinctly and eloquently in the Book of Jeremiah: "To whomever I send you, you shall go, and whatever I command you, you shall speak" (Jer 1:7). In brief, the prophet is the ambassador or messenger of God, and his/her sole duty is to deliver the message as given.[8]

(3) *The Message.* Inevitably, the message will vary greatly with time, place, and circumstance; but in most cases, it is for others, and especially for the nation (often its leaders) and the people generally. Often it contains warnings and threats, and sometimes promises and encouragement. There is naturally a predictive element, as messages are mostly oriented to the future, while rooted in the present or past. For the most part, predictions are: (1) morally conditioned, being based upon the covenant between God and Israel; and (2) offer the choice between life and death, with success as the result of obedience and failure as the consequence of disobedience or defiance. At times, the oracles are pronounced absolutely, guaranteeing the future, whether destruction or restoration. Occasionally, they are time-bound, i.e., within a specified period the events described will occur, but often no timetable is given. Even when no conditions—whether moral or temporal—are laid down, they may be implied by the speaker, or assumed by the hearers. A notable case is the flat prediction by the 8th century prophet Micah (Mic 3:12) that Jerusalem would be destroyed. While no specific time is stated, it must be assumed that a limited period was in mind. A century later, certain elders from the time of Jeremiah (Jer 26:18) quote the prediction, not to show

---

[7] For further discussion of Jonah, see further Freedman 1990a:28.

[8] For the prophet as messenger, see Muilenburg 1965; Westermann 1967: 98–128; Ross 1962; and Holladay 1970 (contrast Baltzer 1968; Rendtorff 1962; and Tucker 1978).

that the prophecy was unfulfilled (Jerusalem had not been destroyed) or, much less, to indict Micah as a false prophet for the failure of his prediction, but rather to argue that, as a result of Micah's prophecy, the king (Hezekiah) and the people repented, and hence Yahweh forgave them and spared the city.[9] In other words, the prophet carried out his commission by bringing the word of God to the city and its people. The outcome was left to the interaction of God and people; in this case, it came out differently from what the prophet had said. But it was Micah's message that produced the result, and therefore both he and his message were vindicated as coming from God.

(4) *The Prophet as Wonder-worker.* This was a distinctive aspect of prophetic behavior in certain cases only, and it is not clear whether it was regarded as important for a prophet to demonstrate such powers, or whether these were more or less incidental and associated with certain charismatic personalities. Thus, miracles are clearly and strongly associated with prophets such as Moses, Samuel, and especially Elijah and Elisha, as well as with Isaiah among the so-called writing prophets; however, there are many prophets with little or no such connection, for example, Jeremiah, Amos, Hosea, and Micah. With Ezekiel, strange things happen to the prophet and he has extraordinary extra-sensory experiences, but these are hardly in the same category with the popular healing and feeding miracles associated with Moses and the period of the Exodus-wanderings or with Elijah and Elisha at a later time. Certainly they were not obligatory, and such miracles seem to be attached to unusual charismatic individuals who were also prophets, but not necessarily to the role or office of prophet.[10] In the case of Moses, the numerous signs and wonders and miraculous powers attributed to him are designed to strengthen

---

9 For further discussion of the Micah prophecy in the book of Jeremiah, see Hillers 1984:8–9. Note also Fishbane 1985:458–60.

10 In later Jewish and early Christian tradition, however, greater importance is attached to miracles as a sign of prophetic status, e.g., Ben Sira's treatment of Elijah (48:1–14) and the New Testament gospels (e.g., Mark 6:14–16 and Luke 9:7–9). See discussion in Barton 1986:99–102.

and confirm his claims to having received an authentic and authoritative message from God. These are especially important in his confrontations with the pharaoh of Egypt and his magicians. Miracles also serve to validate the status of other prophets and fulfill their missions and messages.

(5) *Success and Failure.* On the whole, the results of the prophetic experience were themselves unpredictable. Success or failure on the part of individual prophets hardly affects their status as true prophets of God. In fact, there is almost a reverse—even perverse—correlation between authenticity and success. The greatest of the prophets enjoyed comparatively little success in their lives, as, for example, the bitter outburst of Jeremiah (e.g., Jer 25) attests. On the other hand, prophets such as Samuel and Elisha are reported to have met with success in carrying out their missions. With prophets such as Elijah, and perhaps Isaiah, the results are mixed, as may also be the case for Amos, Hosea, and Micah. Ultimately, they were all recognized as true prophets, not because the leaders and the people heeded their words (often they did not), but because they faithfully reported what they heard from the mouth of God, regardless of the consequences for themselves and the people to whom they delivered the message.

True and False Prophecy

One of the most difficult and disturbing problems that confronted prophets and their listeners in ancient Israel was the question of true and false prophets.[11] This was a vital issue on which the profession itself hung in the balance. Indeed, where the survival of the nation was at stake, it was of utmost importance to distinguish true from false. This was no mere academic exercise, but required the best judgment of leaders and people alike. The Book of Deuteronomy offers rules of procedure to decide the issue

---

[11] On false prophecy/prophetic conflict in general, see, e.g., Quell 1952; Lindblom 1962:210–15; Osswald 1962; Crenshaw 1971 and 1976; Hossfeld and Meyer 1973; Sanders 1977; De Vries 1978; Carroll 1979; Long 1982; and Wilson 1984:67–80.

of truth and falsehood among prophets. There are two basic principles, both practical and applicable, but not in all cases:

(1) If the prophet speaks in the name of and delivers messages from another god or other gods, then he is automatically condemned for apostasy and must be put to death. (Deut 18:20)

(2) If the prophet makes a prediction and in due course the prediction is not fulfilled, that is, what is predicted does not come to pass, then the prophet is judged to be false, and is to be executed (Deut 18:20, 22).

As typical or representative rules, these examples are interesting and of value. While certain obvious cases would be subject to decision and action, it is clear that many others would not (see below). As for the guidelines themselves, it seems clear that, if enforced, these would eliminate prophets of other gods such as Baal or Asherah mentioned in the story of the contest at Mt. Carmel in the days of Elijah (1 Kgs 18:17–40). Even with the elimination of such false prophets, there still remains a large group of prophets of Yahweh to be tested. The second rule would apply to this group. At first sight, a simple test of prediction as an indicator of reliability would seem to be quite feasible. The group could then be divided between those whose predictions came to pass and those whose predictions proved false.

However, the often complex circumstances of real life make matters much more difficult, since there could be (and no doubt were) numerous exceptions on both sides—for example, false prophets who occasionally made true predictions (the law of averages being in their favor), and true prophets who occasionally put forth false ones. Concerning the latter, we possess both the historical data for comparison to the prophetic record and, in some cases, later prophetic testimony. Both came into play in our discussion of Micah's prophecy concerning the destruction of Jerusalem (see above). Here we see how a prophecy could be effective (thereby confirming the prophet's claim and status) in producing events that undercut the prediction itself. Precisely because Micah's prophecy brought about a change in people's lives, its prediction was reversed. In this case, non-fulfillment: (1) is part of the process of effective prophecy; (2) confirms the prophet as authentic; and (3) fulfills the higher and larger purpose of God, while at the same time contradicting the prediction. So non-fulfillment in and of itself is not indicative: it neither proves nor disproves anything. One could go on to say that a century later the prophetic warning was rejected, thus initiating a new chain of interacting events. This time the prediction would be fulfilled in the destruction of the city. Thus, the second time around the prophet Micah was vindicated as true (although it may be questioned whether he could have been thinking more than 100 years ahead of his time). In fact, the second guideline in Deuteronomy requires a relatively short time limit for the prophecy's fulfillment; otherwise, the rule would be useless in deciding whether a contemporary prophet was true or false. If we had to wait 100 years or more to judge the validity of a particular prediction, then the rule would be next to worthless in ascertaining the truth or falseness of a prophet's current message (for that matter, the prophet would be dead before his audience could make the proper determination!).

We have another case in the Book of Ezekiel, in which the prophet concedes that an earlier prophecy about the capture of Tyre by Nebuchadnezzar did not come out as predicted (Ezek 29:17–20; compare earlier 26:7–21). Here the prophet himself acknowledges that his earlier prediction did not come to pass. Except for his concession that he was somehow mistaken, Ezekiel obviously would not agree with the seemingly reasonable judgment—at least by Deuteronomic standards—that he was (by implication) a false prophet. His task and responsibility is to proclaim the word of God. What happens afterwards is God's decision, and he is certainly not bound by earlier predictions. So Ezekiel would in effect reject the (second) Deuteronomic rule. The relationship between Yahweh and the prophets of ancient Israel was undoubtedly more complex than a single rule like the one mentioned above could allow for, and the fulfillment or non-fulfillment of predictions cannot be employed in some simplistic way to distinguish true from false prophets.

Nevertheless, it was absolutely obligatory for Israel to determine who was true and who was false. So much hinges upon it because, not only must the people listen to and obey the true prophet(s), they must at the same time reject the false prophet and what he proclaims. As we have shown, however, the Deuteronomic rules are not practical in certain situations; thus, the jury must find other means of determination. In the end, the decision cannot wait for all the returns to come in, so the deciding vote must be based upon other factors. The chief one, after the basic test of orthodoxy (in the name of which god does the prophet speak?), must be the impact the prophet makes on his audience: his honesty, his courage, his reliability—the ability to make real to his listeners the experience and message of God. There can be confirmation and vindication at a later time, sometimes much later (and in some cases, even too late).

Under the circumstances, and especially when confronted with hard choices—for example, surrender to the Assyrians or resistance in the days of Hezekiah, or the same choice with the Babylonians 100 years later—it was not easy to tell which prophets were true and which were false. The famous case of conflict between Jeremiah and Hananiah in the last days of Judah and Jerusalem (Jer 28–29) exposes the difficulty and explains why the level of bitterness and distress was so high among the prophets.[12] Jeremiah knew firmly who was true and who was false, but how could he prove his case or convince his audience with a message that was considerably less palatable than the comforting words of his rival? During the crisis, neither Deuteronomic rule could be applied satisfactorily: according to external and formal criteria, Hananiah was as much a Yahwist as Jeremiah. His oracles were prefaced with the obligatory "Thus says Yahweh," just as were those of his canonical counterpart. Only time could tell which of the two prophets was right about the political picture and what course the history of a helpless Judah would take under the powerful Babylonians. The later Deuteronomistic editors/redactors already knew the outcome and so included this story of prophetic confrontation in order to bolster the authority of Jeremiah. After

---

[12] For Jeremiah and the false prophets, see Overholt 1970; Meyer 1977; and Lys 1979. Note also the recent commentaries of Holladay (1989:111–30) and Carroll (1986:537–50).

all, we have no book of the prophecies of Hananiah. The issue
between the two prophets was resolved dramatically within the year
when Jeremiah's prediction of Hananiah's death (a clear sign of
divine disfavor) came true; consequently, the latter's optimistic
prophecies about the return of the exiles proved false.

But there undoubtedly were many other prophets (of whom we
have no record) making other claims, thus confusing and
complicating the issue. No wonder the canonical prophets
complain long and loud about the false brethren in their midst. To
be sure, many of the latter, like Hananiah, were sincere, decent
men and women, who believed as firmly as the true prophets that
they were called of God and had received the true word of the
deity through the channels open to them. In a different age and
climate of opinion, one might conclude that the differences were
matters of degree and not essence, and that to a certain extent all
prophets may be called false; that is, inevitably they distort what
they hear and mingle their own thoughts and impressions with
those received from the outside. All honest persons should not
only be tolerated, but listened to so that the public (and the
leadership) might be in a better position to make fateful decisions.
But that is not the way it was in the 8th–6th centuries BCE within
Israel and Judah, and not in the Bible. The dividing line may be
narrow, but it is sharp, and prophets land on one side or the other.
The smaller handful belong to the truth, while the rest fall by the
wayside.

The Ethics of Prophetic Religion

We can distinguish two major historical phases or periods of
prophetic activity and discern an evolution in thought and
perception. While there are constant elements that connect and
unite all the prophets, there are also detectable changes and
differences in emphases and perspectives.

The first historical period would begin with Samuel and his
band of followers and extend to the time of Elijah and Elisha and
their disciples the "sons of the prophets." The second would
encompass the so-called literary prophets from the early 8th

century to the end of the prophetic canon in the 6th or 5th
century BCE.

From beginning to end, the stress in prophetic utterance is on
the ethical dimension of biblical religion and how it affects the
well-being of the nation and its individual members. Over against
the cultic domain of the priests, the prophets stress the moral
demands of the deity and the ethical requirements of the
covenant. There is no necessary conflict between ethical sensitivity
and engagement in the cult, as the whole prophetic tradition and
record show—from Samuel who functioned as priest and prophet,
through Jeremiah and Ezekiel (whose priestly and prophetic
callings are attested), to Haggai, Zechariah and Malachi—all were
heavily involved with cultic, as well as with personal and social
behavior.[13] The survival and success of the community depend
more on the righteousness of the nation, than on the cultic
activities of the priests or the military-political/socio-economic
exploits of the king and his coterie. These emphases translate into
personal moral standards for the individual, and higher ethical
requirements for the nation as a whole. Each person has a grave
two-fold responsibility: (1) to be obedient to the commands or
demands of God, and (2) to cooperate with others in order to
ensure that the level of conformance and performance on the part
of all is commensurate. The first requirement was unwavering and
unswerving: devotion to the one God beside whom there was no
other (at least no other worthy of consideration as such). So the
battle against idolatry and apostasy was waged unremittingly
throughout the whole biblical period, and the leaders in the
struggle were the prophets. Second to this, and equally difficult
and important, was the obligation to one's neighbor and to the
community as a whole. On these two foundations (both of which
are summed up in the decalogue), combining individual and
social/community responsibilities, the prophetic message was
formed and formulated. The prophets never ceased to propound

---

[13] On the question of the prophets and the cult, see the seminal discussion
of Mowinckel 1923 (English translation of chapter one [pp. 3–29] in Petersen
1987:74–98); Johnson 1962; Jeremias 1970; and the essay of R. Murray in
Coggins, Phillips, and Knibb 1982:200–16.

the elementary and basic truths about biblical religion and the relationship of God to his people.

With the prophets of the 8th century (the beginning of our second phase), there was an important shift, although the basic truths remained unchanged. The same requirements and standards were upheld and applied even more sharply to an Israel prone to defection and default. With the appearance of the then great world powers (neo-Assyria in the 8th–7th centuries and neo-Babylonia toward the end of the 7th and on into the 6th century), the question of the survival of those smaller nations to their west (Israel, Judah, and their neighbors) became acute. The prophets raise the issue sharply and in a new way for the first time. There is also a larger perspective on the world scene and the authority of Yahweh as ruler of the nations.[14] The place of Israel and Judah in the larger picture is defined, and a theory of world order with an accompanying time-frame is adumbrated. The implications of a single God ruling the universe, but attached by special ties to one small nation (or two kingdoms), are developed. The danger and threats to the people of God are portrayed in greater relief, as also are the hopes and promises of the future, in which a restored and revealed Israel will take its place among the nations in a harmonious resolution of conflicts to form the Peaceable Kingdom. The ultimate vision encompasses all nations and peoples with a special place for Israel, still obligated by essential covenant stipulations, but a leader and model for all others (e.g., Isa 2:1–4//Micah 4:1–4).[15] Personal faith and morality are at the core of prophetic religion, but the implications and ramifications are social, national, and ultimately world wide.

---

[14] See further comment in Andersen and Freedman 1989:89–97. For Neo-Assyrian influence on the prophets of the period, via imperial administration and the use of propaganda, see especially Holladay 1970 and Machinist 1983.

[15] On the internationalism derived from these and other similar passages, see Orlinsky 1970.

The Prophet as Intercessor

In addition to the primary task of the prophet as messenger and spokesman for God, mention should also be made of another at least equally important role: intercessor on behalf of the people of God.[16] Normally we think of the priests as serving in that capacity, offering up prayers and sacrifices to God on the people's behalf—especially the role of the High Priest on the Day of Atonement, restoring harmony in the relationship between God and people through ritual, sacrifice, and prayer. At the same time, we recognize the work of the priests in providing instruction and information about appropriate behavior, including moral and ethical precepts, as well as cultic and ritual ones. In the same manner, prophets may exercise the role of intercessor, only in a different context; the ultimate role of intercessor is restricted in the Bible to a very limited group. Jeremiah (Jer 15:1) mentions two intercessors, Moses and Samuel, while confirming that God himself has denied that role to him. Of all the other prophets, only Amos claims to have interceded with God on behalf of his people (Amos 7:1–6); so the total number of intercessors is three. We might also mention the patriarch Abraham, who interceded in behalf of Abimelech (Gen 20:7, 17) and in some fashion for the people of Sodom and Gomorrah (Gen 18:16–33). However, questions remain concerning this episode: Did Abraham intercede on behalf of the guilty, or only insist that the righteous should not be punished with the guilty? For fear of confusing the two groups, did he insist that it would be better to spare the city for the sake of the righteous in it? In any case, he was unsuccessful since the cities and their inhabitants were destroyed, with the sole exception of Lot and his family.

The most dramatic case of intercession is that of Moses in the episode of the Golden Calf (Exodus 32). Against the divine decision to destroy his people, Moses insists (indeed he

---

16 On the prophet as intercessor, see Rhodes 1977; Balentine 1984; Barton 1986:102–3; and Muffs 1992. For what follows (intercession and God's repentance), see especially the fuller discussion in Andersen and Freedman 1989:638–79 ("Excursus: When God Repents" [by Freedman]).

commands) that God repent (Hebrew *šûb...wĕhinnāḥēm*, v. 12) and spare his people; this God does. The narrative is unique in its use of the terms for repentance on the lips of a human being; only Moses has the audacity to demand a change of heart on the part of the deity. Such boldness may be explained by the uniquely special and intimate relationship between him and Yahweh; thus, only he could command repentance on the part of God and get away with it, as the text reports. Israel is spared. The only other passage in which God is commanded to repent is a variant poetic version of the same event in Psalm 90 (v. 13). It is not accidental or incidental that this is the only psalm in the Bible directly attributed to Moses.

Whether Samuel was a successful intercessor or not is less clear. In the one recorded instance where he may have undertaken such a task (1 Sam 15:10–34), he apparently did not succeed; that was when God informed Samuel that he had not only repented (*nḥm*) that he had made Saul king, but had finally and irrevocably rejected him as the chosen king of Israel.

The only other instance of prophetic intercession recorded in the Bible is found in the Book of Amos (chap. 7). Following each of the first two visions (7:1–6), Amos intercedes—somewhat more politely than did Moses—and succeeds. Twice God repents and suspends the threatened judgment (7:3, 6). Unlike the episode of the Golden Calf, these are literally "non-events," strictly between prophet and deity, because the success of the prophet insures that nothing happens: divine judgment is not carried out. The reports make for a dramatic initiation of the prophet's career, but otherwise are of little consequence and, as Amos reports, make no impact on the people, who continue to provoke the wrath of Yahweh. Thus with the second pair of visions (7:7–9 and 8:1–3), God assures Amos that he (God) will not swerve from the path of condemnation and punishment.

Because of his inspiration, leadership, and (ultimately) his power of intercession (which he did not hesitate to exercise), Moses remains the unique model of a prophet in the Hebrew Bible. The closing words of the Book of Deuteronomy reflect this singularity: "There has not arisen a prophet since in Israel like Moses, whom Yahweh knew face to face" (34:10).

Works Consulted

Albright, W. F.

    1961   *Samuel and the Beginnings of the Prophetic Movement.* The Samuel H. Goldenson Lecture, 1961. Cincinnati: Hebrew Union College. (Repr. in Orlinsky 1969, Pp. 149–76.)

Andersen, F. I., and D. N. Freedman

    1989   *Amos.* AB 24A. New York: Doubleday.

Balentine, S. E.

    1984   "The Prophet as Intercessor: A Reassessment." *JBL* 103:161–73.

Baltzer, K.

    1968   "Considerations Regarding the Office and Calling of the Prophet." *HTR* 61:567–81.

    1975   *Die Biographie der Propheten.* Neukirchen-Vluyn: Neukirchener.

Barton, J.

    1986   *Oracles of God. Perceptions of Ancient Prophecy in Israel after the Exile.* Oxford/New York: Oxford University Press.

Berger, P.

    1963   "Charisma and Religious Innovation: The Social Location of Israelite Prophecy." *American Sociological Review* 28:940–50.

Birch, B. C.

    1976   *The Rise of the Israelite Monarchy: The Growth and Development of 1 Samuel 7–15.* SBLDS 27. Missoula: Scholars Press.

Blenkinsopp, J.

    1983   *A History of Prophecy in Israel.* Philadelphia: Westminster.

Boecker, H. J.

1969 *Die Beurteilung der Anfänge des Königtums in den deuteronomistischen Abschnitten des I. Samuelbuches. Ein Beitrag zum Problem des 'Deuteronomistischen Geschichtswerks'*. WMANT 31. Neukirchen-Vluyn: Neukirchener.

Buss, M. J.

1982 "An Anthropological Perspective Upon Prophetic Call Narratives." Pp. 9–30 in Culley and Overholt 1982.

Carroll, R. P.

1979 *When Prophecy Failed: Reactions and Responses to Failure in the Old Testament Prophetic Traditions*. London: SCM.

1986 *Jeremiah*. OTL. Philadelphia: Westminster.

Černý, J.

1962 "Egyptian Oracles." Pp. 35–48 in *A Saite Oracle Papyrus from Thebes in the Brooklyn Museum [Papyrus Brooklyn 47.218.3]*, ed. and trans. Richard A. Parker. Providence: Brown University.

Childs, B. S.

1974 *The Book of Exodus*. OTL. Philadelphia: Westminster.

Clements, R. E.

1965 *Prophecy and Covenant*. SBT 43. Naperville, IL: Allenson.

1975 *Prophecy and Tradition*. Atlanta: John Knox.

1977 "Patterns in the Prophetic Canon." Pp. 42–55 in Coats and Long 1977.

Coats, G. W.

1988 *Moses: Heroic Man, Man of God*. JSOTSup 57. Sheffield: JSOT Press.

Coats, G. W., and B. O. Long, eds.

1977 *Canon and Authority. Essays in Old Testament Religion and Theology*. Philadelphia: Fortress.

Coggins, R., A. Phillips, and M. Knibb, eds.

1982 *Israel's Prophetic Tradition. Essays in Honour of Peter R. Ackroyd.* Cambridge: Cambridge University Press.

Crenshaw, J.

1971 *Prophetic Conflict. Its Effect upon Israelite Religion.* BZAW 124. Berlin: de Gruyter.

1976 "False Prophecy." Pp. 701–2 in *IDBSup.*

Crüsemann, F.

1978 *Der Widerstand gegen das Königtum. Die antiköniglichen Texte des Alten Testamentes und der Kampf um den fruhen israelitischen Staat.* Neukirchen-Vluyn: Neukirchener.

Culley, R. C., and Overholt, T. W., eds.

1982 *Anthropological Perspectives on Old Teatament Prophecy.* Semeia 21. Chico, CA: Scholars Press.

De Vries, S. J.

1978 *Prophet Against Prophet: The Role of the Micaiah Narrative (1 Kings 22) in the Development of Early Prophetic Tradition.* Grand Rapids: Eerdmans.

Ellermeier, F.

1968 *Prophetie in Mari und Israel.* Theologische und orientalistiche Arbeiten 1. Herzberg am Harz: Erwin Jungfer.

Ellis, M. de Jong

1989 "Observations on Mesopotamian Oracles and Prophetic Texts: Literary and Historiographic Considerations." *JCS* 41:127–86.

Emerton, J. A., ed.

1980 *Prophecy. Essays Presented to Georg Fohrer on his Sixty-fifth Birthday, 6 September 1980.* BZAW 150. Berlin and New York: de Gruyter.

Engnell, I.

1969   "Prophets and Prophetism in the Old Testament." Pp.
        123–79 in his *A Rigid Scrutiny. Critical Essays on the Old
        Testament.* Trans. from Swedish (1962) by J. T. Willis.
        Nashville: Vanderbilt University Press.

Evans, W. E.

1983   "An Historical Reconstruction of the Emergence of
        Israelite Kingship and the Reign of Saul." Pp. 61–77 in
        *Scripture in Context II. More Essays on the Comparative
        Method,* ed. W. W. Hallo, J. C. Moyer, and L. G. Perdue.
        Winona Lake: Eisenbrauns.

Fischer, G.

1989   *Jahwe unser Gott. Sprache, Aufbau und Erzähltechnik in der
        Berufung des Mose (Ex 3–4).* OBO 91. Freiburg: Universi-
        tätsverlag; Göttingen: Vandenhoeck & Ruprecht.

Fishbane, M.

1985   *Biblical Interpretation in Ancient Israel.* Oxford:
        Clarendon.

Fohrer, G.

1967   *Studien zur alttestamentlichen Prophetie (1949–1965).*
        BZAW 99. Berlin: Töpelmann.

1974–77 *Die Propheten des Alten Testaments,* 7 vols. Gutersloh:
        Mohn.

Freedman, D. N.

1990a   "Did God Play a Dirty Trick on Jonah at the End?" *Bible
        Review* 6/4:26–31.

1990b   "Confrontations in the Book of Amos." *The Princeton
        Seminary Bulletin,* n.s., 11:240–52.

Fritz, V., K. F. Pohlmann, and H. C. Schmitt

1989   *Prophet und Prophetenbuch. Feschrift für Otto Kaiser zum 65.
        Geburtstag.* BZAW 185. Berlin and New York: de
        Gruyter.

Gitay, Y.

1981 *Prophecy and Persuasion: A Study of Isaiah 40–48.* Forum Theologicae Linguisticae 14. Bonn: Linguistica Biblica.

1991 *Isaiah and his Audience: The Structure and Meaning of Isaiah 1–12.* SSN 30. Assen: Van Gorcum.

Gottwald, N. K.

1964 *All the Kingdoms of the Earth. Israelite Prophecy and International Relations in the Ancient Near East.* New York: Harper and Row.

Gressmann, H.

1913 *Moses und seine Zeit. Ein Kommentar zu den Mose-Sagen.* FRLANT 18. Göttingen: Vandenhoeck & Ruprecht.

Habel, N.

1965 "The Form and Significance of the Call Narratives." *ZAW* 77:297–323.

Hackett, J. A.

1980 *The Balaam Text from Deir ʿAlla.* HSM 31. Chico, CA: Scholars Press.

Haran, M.

1977 "From Early to Classical Prophecy: Continuity and Change." *VT* 27:385–97.

Henry, M.-L.

1969 *Prophet und Tradition. Versuch einer Problemstellung.* BZAW 116. Berlin: de Gruyter.

Herrmann, S.

1976 *Ursprung und Funktion der Prophetie im alten Israel.* Opladen: Westdeutscher Verlag.

Heschel, A. J.

1962 *The Prophets.* New York: Harper and Row.

Hillers, D. R.

1984 *Micah.* Hermeneia. Philadelphia: Fortress.

Hoftizer, J., and G. van der Kooij

1976   *Aramaic Texts from Deir ʿAlla.* Documenta et Monumenta Orientis Antiqui, 19. Leiden: Brill.

1991   *The Balaam Text from Deir ʿAlla Re-Evaluated: Proceedings of the International Symposium held at Leiden 21–24 August 1989.* Leiden: Brill.

Holladay, J. S.

1970   "Assyrian Statecraft and the Prophets of Israel." *HTR* 63:29–51. (Repr. in Petersen 1987, pp. 122–43.)

Holladay, W. L.

1989   *Jeremiah 2.* Hermeneia. Philadelphia: Fortress.

Hölscher, G.

1914   *Die Profeten Untersuchungen zur Religionsgeschichte Israels.* Leipzig: Hinrichs.

Hossfeld, F. L., and I. Meyer

1973   *Prophet gegen Prophet. Eine Analysis der alttestamentlichen Texte zum Thema: Wahre und falsche Propheten.* Biblische Beiträge 9. Fribourg: Schweizerisches Katholisches Bibelwerk.

Huffmon, H. B.

1968   "Prophecy in the Mari Letters." *BA* 31:101–24. (Repr. in *The Biblical Archaeologist Reader* 3, ed. E. F. Campbell and D. N. Freedman. New York: Doubleday, 1970, pp. 199–224.)

1992   "Prophecy (Ancient Near East)." Pp. 477–82 in *ABD* 4. New York: Doubleday.

Jeremias, J.

1970   *Kultprophetie und Geschichtsverkundigung in der späten Königszeit Israels.* WMANT 35. Neukirchen-Vluyn: Neukirchener.

Johnson, A. R.

1962   *The Cultic Prophet in Ancient Israel.* 2d ed. Cardiff: University of Wales.

Kaufman, S. A.

1980   "Review Article: The Aramaic Texts from Deir ʿAlla." *BASOR* 239:71–74.

Koch, K.

1983–84 *The Prophets,* 2 vols. Trans. M. Kohl from *Die Propheten I: Assyriche Zeit* and *Die Propheten II: Babylonisch-persische Zeit* (Stuttgart, 1978). Philadelphia: Fortress.

Kselman, J. S.

1985   "The Social World of the Israelite Prophets: A Review Article." *RelSRev* 11.2:120–29.

Lanczkowski, G.

1960   *Altägyptischer Prophetismus.* ÄA 4. Wiesbaden: Harrassowitz.

Layton, S. C.

1992   "Whence Comes Balaam? Num 22,5 Revisited." *Biblica* 73:32–61.

Leclant, J.

1968   "Éléments pour une étude de la divination dans l'Égypte pharaonique." Pp. 1–23 in *La divination, Tome Premier,* ed. André Caquot and Marcel Leibovici. "Rites et pratiques religieuses." Paris: Presses Universitaires de France.

Lemaire, A.

1985   "L'inscription de Balaam trouvée à Deir ʿAlla: epigraphie." Pp. 313–25 in *Biblical Archaeology Today. Proceedings of the International Congress on Biblical Archaeology. Jerusalem, April, 1984.* Jerusalem: Israel Exploration Society.

Levine, B. A.

1985　"The Balaam Inscriptions from Deir ʿAlla: Historical Aspects." Pp. 326–39 in *Biblical Archaeology Today. Proceedings of the International Congress on Biblical Archaeology. Jerusalem, April, 1984.* Jerusalem: Israel Exploration Society.

Lindblom, J.

1962　*Prophecy in Ancient Israel.* Oxford: Blackwell.

Loewe, M., and C. Blacker, eds.

1981　*Oracles and Divination.* Boulder, CO: Shambhala.

Long, B.

1972　"Prophetic Call Traditions and Reports of Visions." *ZAW* 84:494–500.

1976　"Reports of Visions Among the Prophets." *JBL* 95:353–65.

1977　"Prophetic Authority as Social Reality." Pp. 3–20 in Coats and Long 1977.

1982　"Social Dimensions of Prophetic Conflict." Pp. 31–53 in Culley and Overholt 1982.

Lys, D.

1979　"Jérémie 28 et la problème du faux prophète ou la circulation du sens dans le diagnostic prophétique." *Revue d'histoire et de philosophie religieuses* 59:453–82.

Machinist, P.

1983　"Assyria and its Image in First Isaiah." *JAOS* 103:719–37.

Malamat, A.

1980　*Mari and the Bible. A Collection of Studies.* 2d ed. Jerusalem: Hebrew University.

1987　"A Forerunner of Biblical Prophecy: The Mari Documents." Pp. 33–52 in *Ancient Israelite Religion. Essays in Honor of Frank Moore Cross,* ed. P. D. Miller, P. D. Hanson, and S. D. McBride. Philadelphia: Fortress.

1989   *Mari and the Early Israelite Experience.* The Schweich Lectures of the British Academy, 1984. Oxford: Oxford University Press.

Mayes, A. D. H.

1977   "The Period of the Judges and the Rise of the Monarchy." Pp. 285–331 in *Israelite and Judaean History,* ed. J. H. Hayes and J. M. Miller. Philadelphia: Westminster.

Mays, J. L., and P. J. Achtemeier, eds.

1987   *Interpreting the Prophets.* Philadelphia: Fortress.

McKane, W.

1979   "Prophecy and the Prophetic Literature." Pp. 163–88 in *Tradition and Interpretation: Essays by Members of the Society for Old Testament Study,* ed. G. W. Anderson. Oxford: Clarendon.

1982   "Prophet and Institution." *ZAW* 94:251–66.

Meeks, W. A.

1967   *The Prophet-King: Moses Traditions and the Johannine Christology.* NovTSup 14. Leiden: Brill.

Merrill, A. L., and T. W. Overholt, eds.

1977   *Scripture in History and Theology: Essays in Honor of J. Coert Rylaarsdam.* PTMS 17. Pittsburgh: Pickwick.

Mettinger, T. N. D.

1976   *King and Messiah: The Civil and Sacral Legitimation of the Israelite Kings.* ConBOT 8. Lund: Gleerup.

Meyer, I.

1977   *Jeremia und die falschen Propheten.* OBO 13. Göttingen: Vandenhoeck & Ruprecht.

Miller, J. M. and J. H. Hayes

1986   *A History of Ancient Israel and Judah.* Philadelphia: Westminster.

Moran, W. L.

1969   "New Evidence from Mari on the History of Prophecy."
        Biblica 50:15–56.

Mowinckel, S.

1923   *Psalmenstudien III. Kultprophetie und prophetische Psalmen.*
        Skrifter utgit av Videnskapsselskapet i Kristiania II.
        Historisk-Filosofisk Klasse, 1922, 1. Bind, No. 1.
        Kristiania: Jacob Dybwad. (Trans. of chap. 1 [pp. 3–29]
        in Petersen 1987:74–98.)

1946   *Prophecy and Tradition. The Prophetic Books in the Light of
        the Study of the Growth and History of the Tradition.* Oslo:
        Jacob Dybwad.

Muffs, Y.

1992   "Who Will Stand in the Breach? A Study of Prophetic
        Intercession." Pp. 9–48 in his *Love & Joy: Law, Language
        and Religion in Ancient Israel.* New York and Jerusalem:
        Jewish Theological Seminary.

Muilenburg, J.

1965   "The 'Office' of the Prophet in Ancient Israel." Pp. 74–
        97 in *The Bible in Modern Scholarship,* ed. J. P. Hyatt.
        Nashville: Abingdon.

Noort, E.

1977   *Untersuchungen zum Gottesbescheid in Mari.* AOAT 202.
        Neukirchen-Vluyn: Neukirchener.

Nougayrol, J., ed.

1966   *La divination en Mésopotamia ancienne et dans les régions
        voisines.* XIVᵉ Rencontre Assyriologique Internationale
        (Strasbourg, 2–6 juillet 1965). Paris: Presses Universi-
        taires de France.

1968   "La divination babylonienne." Pp. 25–81 in *La divina-
        tion, Tome Premier,* ed. A. Caquot and M. Leibovici.
        "Rites et pratiques religieuses." Paris: Presses Universi-
        taires de France.

Orlinsky, H., ed.

1969   *Interpreting the Prophetic Tradition: The Goldenson Lectures 1955–66.* New York: Ktav.

1970   "Nationalism-Universalism and Internationalism in Ancient Israel." Pp. 206–36 in *Translating and Understanding the Old Testament. Essays in Honor of Herbert Gordon May,* ed. H. T. Frank and W. L. Reed. Nashville: Abingdon.

Osswald, E.

1962   *Falsche Prophetie im Alten Testament.* Sammlung gemeinverständlicher Vorträge und Schriften aus dem Gebiet der Theologie und Religionsgeschichte 237. Tübingen: Mohr.

1984   "Aspekte neuerer Prophetenforschung." *TLZ* 109:641–50.

Overholt, T. W.

1970   *The Threat of Falsehood. A Study in the Theology of the Book of Jeremiah.* SBT, 2d ser. 16. Naperville, IL: Allenson.

1977   "Jeremiah and the Nature of the Prophetic Process." Pp. 129–50 in Merrill and Overholt 1977.

1979   "Commanding the Prophets: Amos and the Problem of Prophetic Authority." *CBQ* 41:517–32.

1986   *Prophecy in Cross-Cultural Perspective. A Sourcebook for Biblical Researchers.* SBLSBS 17. Atlanta: Scholars Press.

1989   *Channels of Prophecy. The Social Dynamics of Prophetic Activity.* Minneapolis: Fortress.

1990   "Prophecy in History: The Social Reality of Intermediation." *JSOT* 48:3–29. (A critical evaluation of the recent work of Auld and Carroll on the prophet as poet. Note also the response of the latter two scholars in this same issue.)

Parker, S. B.

1978   "Possession Trance and Prophecy in Pre-Exilic Israel." *VT* 28:271–85.

Perlitt, L.

1971   "Mose als Prophet." *EvT* 31:588–608.

Petersen, D. L.

1977   *Late Israelite Prophecy. Studies in Deutero-Prophetic Literature and in Chronicles.* SBLMS 23. Missoula, MT: Scholars Press.

1981   *The Roles of Israel's Prophets.* JSOTSup 17. Sheffield: JSOT Press.

Petersen, D. L., ed.

1987   *Prophecy in Israel. Search for an Identity.* IRT 10. Philadelphia: Fortress.

Puech, E.

1985   "L'inscription sur plâtre de Tell Deir ʿAlla." Pp. 354–65 in *Biblical Archaeology Today. Proceedings of the International Congress on Biblical Archaeology. Jerusalem, April 1984.* Jerusalem: Israel Exploration Society.

Quell, G.

1952   *Wahre und falsche Propheten: Versuch einer Interpretation.* BFCT 46.1. Gütersloh: Bertelsmann.

Rad, G. von

1965   *Old Testament Theology II: The Theology of Israel's Prophetic Traditions.* Trans. D. M. G. Stalker from *Theologie des Alten Testaments: Bd. II, Die Theologie der prophetischen Überlieferungen Israels* (Munich, 1960). New York: Harper and Row.

Ramot, L.

1972   "Prophétisme." Cols. 811–1222 in *DBSup* 8. Paris: Letouzey et Ane.

Renaud, B.

1986   "La figure prophétique de Moïse en Exode 3,1–4,17." *RB* 93:510–34.

Rendtorff, R.

1962   "Botenformel und Botenspruch." *ZAW* 74:165–77.

Rhodes, A. B.

1977   "Israel's Prophets as Intercessors." Pp. 107–28 in Merrill and Overholt 1977.

Richter, W.

1970   *Die sogenannten vorprophetischen Berufungsberichte. Eine literaturwissenschaftliche Studie zu 1 Sam 9,1—10,16, Ex 3f. und Ri 6, 11b–17. FRLANT* 101. Göttingen: Vandenhoeck & Ruprecht.

Rofé, A.

1979   *The Book of Balaam (Numbers 22:2—24:25).* Jerusalem: Simor. (Hebrew.)

1988   *The Prophetical Stories. The Narratives about the Prophets in the Hebrew Bible: Their Literary Types and History.* Trans. D. Levy from Hebrew, 1982 (with revisions/additions to English version). Jerusalem: Magnes.

Ross, J. F.

1962   "The Prophet as Yahweh's Messenger." Pp. 98–107 in *Israel's Prophetic Heritage,* ed. B. W. Anderson and W. Harrelson. New York: Harper and Row. (Repr. in Petersen 1987:112–21.)

Rowley, H. H.

1945   "The Nature of Old Testament Prophecy in the Light of Recent Study." *HTR* 38:1–38. (Repr. in his *The Servant of the Lord and other Essays on the Old Testament,* 1965, pp. 97–134.)

Sanders, J. A.

1977   "Hermeneutics in True and False Prophecy." Pp. 21–41 in Coats and Long 1977.

Schmid, H.

1968   Mose: Überlieferung und Geschichte. BZAW 110. Berlin: Töpelmann.

Schmitt, A.

1982   Prophetischer Gottesbescheid in Mari und Israel. Eine Strukturuntersuchung. BWANT 6/14. Stuttgart: Kohlhammer.

Tucker, G. M.

1973   "Prophetic Authenticity: A Form Critical Study of Amos 7:10–17." Int 27:423–34.

1978   "Prophetic Speech." Int 32:31–45. (Repr. in Mays and Achtemeier 1987, pp. 27–40.)

1985   "Prophecy and Prophetic Literature." Pp. 325–68 in The Hebrew Bible and its Modern Interpreters, ed. D. A. Knight and G. M. Tucker. Chico, CA: Scholars Press.

Veijola, T.

1977   Das Königtum in der Beurteilung der deuteronomistischen Historiographie. Eine redaktionsgeschichtliche Untersuchung. Annales Academiae Scientarum Fennicae, ser. B, 198. Helsinki: Suomalainen Tiedeakatemia.

Weimar, P.

1980   Die Berufung des Mose. Literaturwissenschaftliche Analyse von Exodus 2,23–5,5. OBO 32. Freiburg: Universitätsverlag; Göttingen: Vandenhoeck & Ruprecht.

Weinfeld, M.

1977   "Ancient Near Eastern Patterns in Prophetic Literature." VT 27:178–95.

Weippert, H., K. Seybold, and M. Weippert

1985   Bieträge zur prophetischen Bildsprache in Israel und Assyrien. OBO 64. Freiburg: Universitätsverlag; Göttingen: Vandenhoeck & Ruprecht.

Weippert, M.

1981 "Assyrische Prophetien der Zeit Asarhaddons und Assurbanipals." Pp. 71–115 in *Assyrian Royal Inscriptions: New Horizons in Literary, Ideological, and Historical Analysis*, ed. F. M. Fales. Orientis antiqvi colletio 17. Rome: Instituto per l'Oriente.

Westermann, C.

1967 *Basic Forms of Prophetic Speech.* Trans. H. C. White from *Grundformen prophetischer Rede*, 1960. Philadelphia: Westminster. (Note also German 5th ed., 1978.)

1987 *Prophetische Heilsworte im Alten Testament.* FRLANT 145. Göttingen: Vandenhoeck & Ruprecht. Trans. as *Prophetic Oracles of Salvation in the Old Testament* (Louisville: Westminster/John Knox, 1991).

Williams, J.

1969 "The Social Location of Israelite Prophecy." *JAAR* 37: 153–65.

Wilson, R. R.

1978 "Early Israelite Prophecy." *Int* 32:3–16. (Repr. in Mays and Achtemeier 1987, pp. 1–13.)

1980 *Prophecy and Society in Ancient Israel.* Philadelphia: Fortress.

1984 *Sociological Approaches to the old Testament.* Philadelphia: Fortress.

Wolff, H.

1955 "Die Hauptprobleme alttestamentlicher Prophetie." *EvT* 16:446–68.

Zimmerli, W.

1965 *The Law and the Prophets. A Study of the Meaning of the Old Testament.* New York: Harper and Row.

1977 "Prophetic Proclamation and Reinterpretation." Pp. 69–100 in *Tradition and Theology in the Old Testament*, ed. D. A. Knight. Philadelphia: Fortress.

1979   *Ezekiel 1*. Hermeneia. Philadelphia: Fortress

MAX WEBER, CHARISMA AND BIBLICAL PROPHECY

Ronald E. Clements

Seen in historical perspective Max Weber's treatment of the concept of charisma has proved to be one of the most wide-ranging and influential of his many insights into the workings of society (Gerth and Wright Mills:245–52; Eisenstadt; Albrow: 171ff.). Not only is this the case on the broad front of the study of sociology of religion, but particularly is it so in regard to its influence upon biblical studies. It is also a somewhat unsettling influence, since Weber himself did not present any very rounded, or complete, interpretation of what he meant by the concept of charisma or how it was perceived by those who responded to the experience of it. Indeed, it could be argued that it is not possible to offer such, since it is more a matter of working inductively and recognizing where such a characterisation applies in particular historical and political situations.

The recognition that a charismatic element has been present in the achievement of certain individuals enables us, in retrospect, to understand why their leadership was so effective. It serves to explain, if only by a broad description, why these individuals were able to command a strong following and why they were able to implement changes that their communities were otherwise reluctant to make. In many of its features such an element of charisma is nebulous and only capable of being loosely defined. It is this lack of definition that has enabled it to be applied in very diverse ways and to a great variety of situations.

Nor should we lose sight of the fact that, in a number of respects, the notion of charisma highlights the uniquely personal, and often unforeseeable, factors that affect historical events (Albrow:172). It has affinities with the emphasis upon the "heroic"

approach to the interpretation of history which held great appeal
to much nineteenth and twentieth century historical writing.

1. Charisma and Kingship

Weber himself did not develop any special separate treatment
of the subject where it could be dealt with comprehensively as a
separate topic for examination. It occurs as part of a wider range of
analyses of social change and the interplay of authority between
individuals and institutions. The modern reader is well served by
the selection and translation of Weber's writings that have a
bearing on the topic made by S. N. Eisenstadt (Eisenstadt, 1968
and Weber, 1963: xxxiiiff.). However, it is important to recognize
that the most significant *locus* where Weber sought to define
charisma and to illustrate its mode of working was presented in less
than a half-dozen pages (Gerth and Wright Mills: 245–52).
Nevertheless, the main principles of its operation are significant
for quite a wide area of Weber's writings.

Our present concern is not primarily to re-examine Weber's
own words on the subject, but rather to consider the way in which
his observations have been understood in relation to Israelite
prophecy. In a rather different connection it is useful to note at
the outset that a wide area where the charismatic authority and
leadership ascribed to individuals has drawn the attention of
biblical scholars concerns the institution of monarchy into the
tribal society of Israel (Malamat, 1981). The narrative stories telling
how this latter development occurred with the figures of Saul and
David make extensive play on authority provided by the
charismatic ideal. Yet it is noteworthy that the primary concern of
such stories is to show how this ideal was properly transferred to
David's descendants in a dynastic succession (cf. Rosenberg, 1986;
Halpern, 1980). By taking for granted the notion that charismatic
authority passed to the divinely designated son and heir, a large
unit of narrative concerning affairs at David's court is aimed at
defending Solomon's claim to be such an heir.

In this fashion the claim to individual charismatic authority
linked to the person of David has been carried over in defense of
the traditional authority of a royal dynasty. At the same time, it

becomes evident that the extent to which Solomon could be properly regarded as entitled to recognition as the legitimate, and divinely appointed, heir of David was widely regarded as questionable. So what has come to be described as "The Succession Document" takes for granted the principle that the Davidic family is the proper channel through which the royal authority of David is to be upheld. In effect the charismatic principle that applies uniquely to David is carried over to the dynasty descended from him and is used both to support the authority of the monarchy as an institution, and the dynasty to which that institution is to be uniquely tied.

The significance of noting these features regarding the applicability of the concept of charisma to the extensive accounts of how Israel acquired a monarchy is twofold: In the first place the accounts support fully the point made by Weber that charismatic authority tends to pass over into a more institutionalized form of authority, in this case that of a royal dynasty. When this happens the strength and authority of the original truly charismatic leadership is significantly changed. This may lead to such a weakening of authority that a continued appeal back to the original charismatic figure may become necessary in order to support the much weaker claims attaching to the dynasty that derived from it. The several short-lived royal dynasties of Israel's Northern Kingdom may serve further as illustrations of this (cf. K. W. Whitelam, 1989:119ff and contrast Alt, 1966:239ff).

2. The Idea of Charisma

In a second consideration concerning the nature of charisma, it is useful to note some remarks by S. N. Eisenstadt in the introduction he offers to his translation of the extracts from Weber's writings on the subject:

> In much of existing sociological literature it has been assumed that a deep chasm exists between the charismatic aspects and the more ordinary, routine aspects of social organization and the organized, continuous life of social institutions—and that Weber himself stressed this dichotomy. It seems to me, however, that this is a mistaken view and that the best clue to understanding Weber's work,

and especially his significance for modern sociology lies in the
attempt to combine the two and to analyze how they are interrelated
in the fabric of social life and the processes of social change.
(Eisenstadt :ix).

It is this point concerning the interrelationship between charismatic and routine aspects of social life and organization that forms
the main feature of this essay and which appears to be fully
substantiated by the remarks already made concerning Israel's
kingship. The stories concerning the dynasty founder's unique
charisma are directed towards defending the organized continuing
life of Israel and Judah under a monarchy.

This observation indicates how the idea of charismatic
leadership is important not simply as a distinctive phenomenon in
its own right, but as part of the recognition of a continuing
interplay between the unique, one-off, leadership of unusual
individuals and the larger group that responds to this. Each
influences the other and acts on the other in ways that form a
necessary part of the social process. I am not simply arguing here
for a more carefully considered sociological use of the term
charisma, set over against its more popular modern use; the more
significant point is that charisma can only be effectively understood
in relation to its opposite, which concerns that which is ordinary,
routine and frequently found (C. Schäfer-Lichtenberger 1995:
24ff).

According to Dirk Käsler, Weber's intellectual development
was strongly influenced by a concern to understand the role of
economic and juridical institutions in governing individual
freedom and the possibility of individual self-realization in a social
setting (Käsler: 127ff.). This raised the question of the interplay
between the authority felt by the individual and that imposed by
the group. It is to this issue that the concept of charisma is
addressed, and, with it, the clearer grasp of its opposite, which is to
be found in that which is routine and everyday. Accordingly, for
any change to be brought about by the work of unique individuals
in the more lasting and commonplace life of the community, the
insights of the charismatic leader need to be "routinized," i.e.

brought to the level of the everyday routine. We can let Weber speak:

> The term "charisma" will be applied to a certain quality of an individual personality by virtue of which he is set apart from ordinary men and treated as endowed with supernatural, superhuman, or at least specifically exceptional powers or qualities. These are such as are not accessible to the ordinary person, but are regarded as of divine origin or as exemplary, and on the basis of them the individual concerned is treated as a leader. In primitive circumstances this peculiar deference is paid to prophets, to people with a reputation for therapeutic or legal wisdom, to leaders in the hunt, and heroes in war. . . . Charismatic authority is thus specifically outside the realm of every-day routine and the profane sphere. (Eisenstadt: 48, 51)

In its pure form charismatic authority has a character specifically foreign to everyday routine structures. The social relationships directly involved are strictly personal, based on the validity and practice of charismatic personal qualities. If this is not to remain a purely transitory phenomenon, but to take on the character of a permanent relationship forming a stable community of disciples or a band of followers or a party organization, it is necessary for the character of charismatic authority to become radically changed. Indeed in its pure form charismatic authority may be said to exist only in the originating process. It cannot remain stable, but becomes either traditionalized or rationalized, or a combination of both (cf. Eisenstadt: 54).

Weber contends that charismatic leadership provides a basis of authority which is short-lived and relatively unstable, and this is fully substantiated in the biblical stories about how kingship became a part of Israel's life. It tended to remain an ideal type of authority, intermittently experienced, but which could later be appealed to in support of relatively weak forms of traditonal authority.

It is also relevant to note that the most powerful manifestations of charisma may often only be truly identified *after the event*. Stories of how this charisma was displayed and experienced by the larger community may then be told in respect to the changes which the charismatically endowed leader helped to bring about. Appeals to his, or her, great charisma, as exemplified by exceptional feats, are therefore made in order to justify changes which would otherwise be questionable, or even vigorously opposed.

3. Prophecy and Charisma

The particular relevance of these remarks to the rather different question concerning how notions of charisma may help towards a better understanding of Israelite prophecy is twofold. On the one hand they show that charismatic authority tended to remain a relatively infrequently experienced and ideal type of authority. On the other hand they show that written records of the major charismatic heroes tended to be utilized in support of more long-lasting patterns of authority vested in institutions. The ideal of divine charisma was appealed to in support of institutions which might otherwise remain weak and insecure. We shall see that this is a relevant point in relation to the need to understand the character and structure of the biblical prophetic writings.

Our immediate concern is with the light that the concept of charisma can shed upon the nature and contribution of prophecy to the development of ancient Israel, and to the formation of a corpus of prophetic writings in the Bible. It is readily apparent that Weber himself, in his important studies of socio-religious development of ancient Judaism, accorded a very prominent place to the activities of the prophets (Weber, 1952; cf. also Weber, 1963:xxxiiiff.). Not surprisingly therefore biblical scholarship has found itself endeavoring to draw insight and support from these observations. However, the emphases that have accompanied these observations have frequently drawn attention to features that were not those singled out by Weber himself. At the same time, it also needs to be recognized that the critical reconstructions of the development of Israelite prophecy upon which Weber drew have undergone very substantial reappraisals in recent years (cf. C. Schäfer-Lichtenberger. 1991:85ff.). Accordingly, several of the features to which Weber devoted special attention should now be regarded in a more critical light.

Several aspects of the activities and achievements of the biblical prophets entitles them to be described properly as charismatic

figures. It is also appropriate to suggest that a closer examination
of Weber's ideas on the subject outside his specific interest in
ancient Judaism serves to illuminate a number of features of
prophecy which have hitherto largely been left aside from
consideration of their charismatic significance.

. We may begin by reconsidering the question of social position
and the functioning of a prophet. It is noteworthy that on these
issues several studies have placed a suprisingly heavy emphasis
upon the psychological aspects of prophetic activity, its alliance
with forms of ecstatic religion, and the socially marginal position
which the prophet occupied within the life of the community
(Wilson:56ff., 62ff.; Lewis:23ff.).

When Weber wrote his essays on ancient Judaism this emphasis
was readily intelligible on account of the attention that the writings
of H. Gunkel and G. Hölscher had drawn to these matters
(Neumann:109ff.). Yet it remains doubtful whether the many
attempts to uncover the psychology of prophecy, which may or may
not be valid in their own ways, have much real bearing on the
question of its charismatic quality as Weber presented the notion.
The fact that a prophet may have behaved in a strange manner,
that he, or she, may have come from an economically weak stratum
of society, or that such prophecies were uttered in a trance-like
state of extreme excitement has little bearing on whether or not
this entitles such figures to be classed as charismatic in the sense in
which Weber employed the term. Fundamentally, Weber's notion
of charisma is to be understood in connection with the qualitative
difference of a relatively few outstanding individuals who are
capable of initiating major social change. Such a notion belongs,
not so much to the unusual behavior displayed by religious
functionaries in a community, but rather to the highly distinctive
attainments of such individuals within the larger group. Also it is a
major feature of the argument presented here that the concept of
charisma is particularly applicable to the canonical prophets of
Israel and Judah on account of the radical positions they adopted
towards the major religious and political institutions of their time.
The "charismatic" authority contrasted with the more traditional
forms of authority vested in these institutions.

In recognizing the appearance and public popularity of a number of "false" prophets the biblical record amply warns us against supposing that the enduring significance of prophecy lay in the manner of its public presentation or reception. The fact that only a tiny handful of prophets have ultimately been accorded canonical status indicates that only a few were thought to manifest the true quality of charisma such as Weber described. This charisma manifested itself through its power to initiate change, to elicit recognition for one individual over against the authority of well established institutions, and to exhibit a distinctiveness of authority which lacked any other explanation save that it derived from a special divine gift.

It would be more appropriate to apply Weber's concept of charisma to explain why some prophets were identified as "true" while others were "false," than to characterize whole groups of practitioners such as mantic prophets as charismatic figures. At the most we should recognize that the latter, because of their social and behavioral distinctiveness, had the potential for being recognized as charismatic figures in the narrower sense. We should certainly note the tendency to draw special attention to the various manifestations and phenomena associated with ecstatic religion. No doubt this is also related to the way in which prophets frequently emerged in society from small communities that had been forced onto the margins of economic and political life. Nevertheless, such observations have only a partial bearing on their being regarded as charismatic figures in the narrowly defined understanding of charismatic uniqueness with which Weber was concerned.

Consequently all attempts to associate the possession of charisma with the psychological eccentricities of prophets, or with their origins from distinct social groups, has only limited significance for the more unique gifts with which they are credited in the biblical records. The charismatic endowment possessed by specifically named prophetic individuals must be linked more directly to the particular religious and political insights which they displayed and to the fundamental changes in the status of religious institutions that they helped to bring about.

4. Charisma and Written Testimony

On the positive side of maintaining the claim that prophets displayed charismatic quality in the sense that Werber regarded as most important, there would appear to be worthwhile insights to be gained. Foremost we must set here the issues relating to an awarenss that a gap exists between our possession of a prophetic book, purporting to derive from the prophet, and that prophet's activity for which we have effectively no other surviving testimony (Clements, 1986, 1990)). The very stimulus towards preserving a written record of a prophet's sayings and actions would seem to have arisen out of a sense that he had shown himself to be a uniquely endowed individual; he possessed charisma.

In the biblical canon of prophecy it is not difficult to see why the beginning of the written preservation of the sayings of certain prophets begins in the eighth century BCE. It is because this was the period when the sister kingdoms of Israel and Judah first began to fall under the ruinous impact of Assyrian imperial expansion. Accordingly, we must ackowledge that the preservation of written prophecy was primarily related to the issues attendant upon this disastrous political experience. So the recognition of the charisma attaching to the work of Amos, Hosea, Isaiah and Micah in the eighth century BCE was inseparably linked to the stance they adopted towards these issues. Their threats and warnings were seen as providing some explanation of the political disasters that overtook Israel and Judah. Other features concerning their religious loyalties and moral insights must be regarded as secondary to this, even though they cannot be dismissed as unimportant.

A second issue concerning the value of using the term charisma in connection with the work of the biblical prophets is closely related to this. It concerns the question of the purpose of preserving the prophets' sayings in written form for future generations to read and ponder. Such action can scarcely have been intended simply as a consequence of lasting interest in the immense political and social turmoil brought about by Mesopotamian political incursions from the eighth to sixth

centuries BCE. It must have been because the prophets' words
provided legitimation for changes which these events brought
about.

This further helps to explain the fact that the canonical shape
of the prophetic writings bears ample evidence that it was more
important to preserve knowledge of the prophet's sayings than to
recall a record of his life. The charisma was not important in itself;
it mattered only in relation to the social and religious changes
which the charismatic individual brought about. The written
prophetic word was looked upon as the authoritative testimony,
which served to explain the cessation of major features of Israel's
and Judah's national life and their replacement by others. It also
provided assurance that a time would come when fundamental
institutions of that national life which had foundered, such as the
Davidic kingship and the Jerusalem temple, would be restored.

The concern to locate such prophecies within the life and work
of specific prophets has arisen precisely because these prophets
were believed to have displayed charisma in the full Weberian
sense. They had foreseen the coming ruin of Israel and Judah and
the great institutions, which had shaped the existence of these
kingdoms. Nor is it at all difficult to see how the fact that Judah
appeared at first to have survived the ruin that befell the Northern
Kingdom in the eighth century produced a strong, but ultimately
disappointed, expectation that the survival of the Davidic
monarchy and the Jerusalem temple would serve to ensure the
political continuance of Judah.

Subsequent events of the sixth century inflicted upon Judah
and Jerusalem by Nebuchadnezzar frustrated all such expectations.
This fact has meant that a further group of prophecies concerning
both kingship and temple has been given great prominence in the
preserved prophetic corpus. Not only have the entire books of
Jeremiah and Ezekiel been shaped by this knowledge, but the
much older collection of Isaiah's prophecies has been substantially
recast and supplemented as a result.

It may also be argued that the complexity of the tensions
inherent in the final shaping of the Deuteronomistic History
(Josh–2 Kgs) are also a result of the frustration of the hopes that

were bound up with the fortunes of the Davidic dynasty and the Jerusalem temple.

That prophecy was vitally important as a medium through which Israel and Judah could interpret, and come to terms with, these tragic events lies in the very nature of charismatic authority. The prophet's claim to be able to speak directly on behalf of God placed him outside the more traditional and rational forms of authority of ongoing religious institutions. He felt no compulsion to submit to them, and did not need to appeal to them for his legitimacy.

However, once the catastrophes which had befallen Israel and Judah lay in the past, these communities needed to restore the credibility of these institutions, which had provided more fixed and stable forms of authority. This was necessary in order for these communities to cope with the routine of everyday life. It is this process of giving credibility to a greatly revised religious order of life which written prophecy could provide. In order to do so it was dependent upon appeal to the original highly respected prophet's words. His special insights and gifts provided the means of substantiating the claims to legitimacy of the new order.

5. Charisma and the Wider Community

Clearly, the charismatic leader would have been nothing without the larger group which existed around him, and to which his message was addressed. In considerable measure it is this group —their needs, their deference to his gifts, their rallying to his banner—which marked him out as an especially important figure. This group, therefore, played a necessary role in the identification and affirmation of the possessor of charisma (Clements, 1986, 1990). It is, however, a qualitatively and functionally different role from that of the charismatic leader. The charismatic leader displays a unique element of authority over the group, whereas the group recognizes itself as having been the recipient and beneficiary of this gift.

An excellent example of this appropriation of the message of a uniquely individual prophet by the concerns and interests of a larger, institutionally related group, is found in the book of the prophet Jeremiah. As is now widely recognized, this prophet's words have been accomodated, in their written form, into an intellectual and religious framework characterized as Deuteronomic, or Deuteronomistic (Herrmann:66ff; Clements, 1993:93ff). So far as we can identify its features this was an influential, and centrally based, reform movement that first emerged during the seventh century in the wake of the intrusions into Israel and Judah which had begun a century earlier.

The thesis that the major prophets of the Hebrew Bible were drawn from socially marginal groups appears largely to have arisen in order to fit such figures into a recognizable pattern, rather than on the basis of substantive evidence. The kind of moral and religious offenses that the prophets accuse their contemporaries of committing and tolerating, are, for the most part, the kinds of offenses which were endemic to Near Eastern society for many centuries. They relate to corruption, abuse of the legal system, greed and oppression, all of which could not have been either newly perceived, or uniquely rampant, problems of Israel and Judah in the eighth to sixth centuries BCE. Thus there is little reason for supposing that opposition to them arose in any very obvious way among the more marginal elements in society.

There would then seem to be little reason for claiming that the major canonical prophets were especially the representatives of marginalized social groups, although we cannot exclude this possibility. Much more important is the point that it was the major central religious and political institutions of Israel and Judah that were threatened with total eclipse as a consequence of the Assyrian and Babylonian interventions and attacks. The words of the major prophets served to provide a basis for renewing and re-asserting the authority of these institutions when their survival was under threat. All the indications are that both Isaiah and Ezekiel came from within a group which stood within the main circles of governmental authority. Even if, as is often argued, such figures as Amos, Hosea and Jeremiah emanated from more peripheral communities, it would appear that their prophecies have been accomodated into the framework of ideas of a more central establishment.

So we can regard much of the prophetic invective as of a relatively conventional nature, even though it was evidently delivered with great intensity and passion. The primary significance of the charismatic insights of the prophets was provided by the broader political scene of the period in which they emerged. This established the need for preserving a written record of their words, rather than as the consequence of a crisis of unprecedented social and moral pressures that their respective communities were experiencing.

If this is a valid observation, then it should lead us to recognize that the charismatic quality of the canonical prophets is primarily to be seen in the connection between their distinctive insights and emphases and the collapse of the political institutions in which they operated. In foretelling the imminent threat of ruin and disaster befalling Israel and Judah the remarkable succession of prophets accurately read the message of their times. Most of their contemporaries failed to do so!

6. Charisma and the Canon of Written Prophecy

Awareness of the nature of the charismatic distinctiveness and individuality of the great prophets is of relevance to the belief that the literary form of prophecy in the Hebrew Bible may be understood as the work of "schools" of prophets. Such views were at one time advocated by a number of Scandinavian scholars and find one of their strongest expression in Engnell's essay "Prophets and Prophetism in the Old Testament (Engnell, 1970).

Engnell rejects the idea that any major distinction can be made between the work of the original prophet and that of his disciples. All prophets are regarded as the leaders of schools and the books ascribed to individual prophets are the products of such schools. Engnell regards it as pointless to try to distinguish between the work of the original prophet and that of his followers. I have consistently remained sceptical about this claim to the existence of prophetic schools, and I think that the term can only be helpful in a much modified sense. To a large extent the importance attached to the notion of charisma, as Weber understood it in relation to individual creativity and situations of social change, could not easily be spread too widely.

Individuality and distinctiveness are of the essence of what constitutes charismatic authority. The belief that schools of prophets existed resolves the question of individual and corporate elements in the formation of the prophetic literature by setting aside the individual aspect of the specific prophetic charisma. It may even suggest that such charisma could be passed on from one prophet to another in a transfer of authority analogous to that of a royal dynasty. Yet there is only minimal evidence that this occurred, and clearly the Hebrew Bible contains no attempt to provide authorisation for such prophetic schools on the model displayed by the monarchy.

On this particular score Weber's special interest in the question of charismatic authority attaching to prophets appears to be a valuable corrective to several assumptions about prophecy that have otherwise had a powerful influence among biblical scholars. In a real measure they help us to recover a greater sense of the individuality and creativity of the great prophets. For Weber, the sense of the prophet's uniqueness, the awareness that he stood apart from other individuals and perceived truths that were hidden from their eyes, was the essence of his task. The idea that a prophetic "office" existed of the kind that meant that a continuing succession of figures occupied the same role may have been true in the sense that cultic officials of such a kind existed in ancient Israel; but it fails to accord with the sense of uniqueness accorded to the named figures of classical prophecy. They were somehow different, and it is this difference that the notion of charisma seeks to explain.

In maintaining a scepticism concerning the existence of significant schools of prophets who maintained a distinct religious identity, we must nevertheless recognize that a prophet's words needed to be remembered and appropriated by the groups that came to surround him. This could not occur without that message being elaborated and subjected to some degree of adaptation and modification. In Weber's terminology it needed to be "routinized." Religious ideals needed to be spelled out in terms of everyday precepts and rules that could be acted upon in an everyday setting. It was in this respect that the kinds of moral and religious invective, that had served to back up the prophet's threats, provided a useful medium of instruction. They enabled prophecy to become detached from the unique and unrepeatable situations in which it had originated and accomodated into a more lasting literature of admonition and assurance and legitimation.

Similarly, since the great prophets had arisen at a time of threat to the estasblished religious institutions of the nation, it became essential that their teaching should be clarified to show what kind of institutions they did support. Since these charismatically endowed prophets had addressed their sayings to situations which witnessed major upheavals in the life of Israel and Judah, it had to be shown in what manner they had interpreted such upheavals. By offering reasons for calamity they were able to demonstrate that the divine government of Israel remained an intelligible belief.

It is in these reasons for calamity that the strength and originality of the prophetic contribution is to be seen. Such reasons included various features of cultic polemic, but most prominenetly of all, they included the giving of priority to moral integrity and commitment to righteousness. It was this emphatic priority that marked the enduring feature of prophetic originality. We should not suppose that the prophets perceived a different kind of moral order from that which shaped the thinking of lawmakers and sages. Rather, the moral and social issues on which they focussed attention were, in large measure, issues which were endemic to a society experiencing the economic and social changes which colored ancient Israel's life. Nevertheless, the prophetic invective placed such a weight of importance upon these moral questions that they took on a new significance as factors by which the entire life of the nation could be seen and judged. To a considerable extent, in the prophetic invective, the historical order was itself seen to be subject to moral judgement. In place of arbitrary and uncontrollable forces, history, with all its vicissitudes, was moralized.

The awareness that the insights of the charismatic prophet marked the experience of catastrophe as a transitional, but necessary, aberration of the divine purpose in specific situations shows how the prophetic charisma did not itself represent a permanent form of authority. Like all charismatic authority, it was temporary and unique to one individual. It could only be effective when its demands were modified and adapted to accomodate to the more lasting religious needs of the people.

7. Charisma and Routinization

Charismatic authority needed to be transformed, by the nature of its own unstable character, into a variety of forms of more traditional authority. The spoken word of the original prophet needed to become the meticulously preserved written word of the prophetic book. In the process, considerable additions and changes needed to be made for the work of routinization to be implemented. The unique and transitory situation which the original prophet had encountered had to be set in a perspective that made it possible for the more enduring and practical needs of the community that respected him to be met.

So there is much in Weber's understanding of the nature of charisma which helps to explain the contents and shaping of the prophetic literature of the Hebrew Bible. The necessity for some form of routinization seems to me to assist, at least in part, in understanding why so much additional material has been incorporated into each of the prophetic books. During the nineteenth century this material came to be classed as "inauthentic" and to be largely set aside in the work of interpretation. However, it is notworthy that this is not the feature of Weber's interpretation of charisma which has most interested biblical scholars. Instead, certain other aspects attaching to the concept have elicited more attention. I might then suggest that Weber's own insights have actually tended, rather ironically, to be routinized in a manner which has exaggerated certain features at the expense of others. It is then open to suggest that it is these latter features which may prove to be more helpful so far as understanding the prophetic literature is concerned.

In particular the inevitability of the tension that Weber pointed to between the original charismatic authority of the prophetic individual and the ongoing life of religious institutions seems to be a helpful one. It describes very well the various interests that have led to the supplementation and editing of the prophetic sayings to form them into books. For the most part this is not the work of individuals who aspired to setting their own prophecies and teachings alongside that of the great charismatic figures. Rather, it should be seen as a work of interpretation and routinization that endeavored to make the insights and messages of the great prophets applicable to the ongoing needs of a larger world of followers.

Furthermore, it seems apparent that the sayings of prophets have frequently been used to serve as a form of legitimation for major shifts in the operation and control of the cultus in Israel. Judaism was forced to accomodate profound departures from the original model it had projected of the Mosaic cultus. The earlier conventional tendency to contrast the acultic, or anti-cultic, stance of the pre-exilic prophets with the more evident pro-cultic interest of the post-exilic ones is largely misinterpreted. The shaping of the canonical corpus of prophecy has endeavored to accomodate both features to a common purpose. This work of canonical shaping and collecting drew upon the words of the prophets as a form of authorization for adopting inevitable and unanticipated changes to this original priestly model of cultic life. The notion of the charismatically endowed prophet provided the essential link in the chain of divine command and human appropriation that made such changes acceptable.

To this degree it is arguable that the Hebrew prophetic writings show as much concern about forms of traditonal authority as about the exclusively charismatic. Perhaps, more precisely, the essential feature is that the very nature of appeals to charismatic authority required that they should be seen in relation to the ongoing, institutional aspects of religion which they challenged. The older picture of an almost inevitable confrontation between prophet and cultus failed to grasp the point that each could only properly function in relation to the other. It was because the cultus was vulnerable to change and obsolescence that it required to be revised and reinvigorated by the input which only the charismatic prophet could provide. Appeals back to the prophetic word of God of the past served to provide a basis of authority by which the less exciting, but more enduringly necessary, religious institutions of the present could be maintained. In general perspective, therefore, it is arguable that Weber's interest in the limitations and instability of all forms of charismatic authority has much to contribute towards a better understanding of the nature of prophecy.

Works Consulted

Albrow, M.

1990   *Max Weber's Construction of Social Theory*. London: Macmillan.

Alt, A.

1966   "The Monarchy in the Kingdoms of Israel and Judah." Pp. 239–59 in *Essays on Old Testament History and Religion*. Oxford: Blackwell.

Clements, R. E.

1982   "The Ezekiel Tradition: Prophecy in a Time of Crisis." Pp. 119–36 in I*srael's Prophetic Tradition*, ed. R. J. Coggins et al. Cambridge: Cambridge University Press. (Repr. as pp. 145–58 in *Old Testament Prophecy. From Oracles to Canon*. [Louisville: Westminster/John Knox, 1995].)

1986   "Prophecy as Literature: A Re-Appraisal." Pp. 56–76 in *The Hermeneutical Quest: Essays in Honor of J. L. Mays for His 65th Birthday*, ed. D. G. Miller, PTMS 4. Allison Park: Pickwick.

1990   "The Prophet and His Editors." Pp. 203–20 in *The Bible in Three Dimensions*, ed. D. J. A. Clines et al. JSOTSup 87. Sheffield: Sheffield Academic Press.

1993   "Jeremiah 1–25 and the Deuteronomistic History." Pp. 93–113 in *Understanding Poets and Prophets. Essays in*

Honour of George Wishart Anderson. JSOTSup 152. Sheffield: Sheffield Academic Press.

Eisenstadt, S. N.

1968   *Max Weber on Charisma and Instituion Building: Selected Papers.* Chicago: University of Chicago Press.

Engnell, I.

1970   "Prophets and Prophetism in the Old Testament." Pp. 123–79 in *Critical Essays on the Old Testament.* London: SPCK.

Gerth, H. H. and C. W. Mills

1948   *From Max Weber: Essays in Sociology.* London: Routledge and Kegan Paul.

Halpern, B.

1980   "The Political Impact of David's Marriages." *JBL* 99:507–28.

Käsler, D.

1988   *Max Weber: An Introduction to His Life and Work.* Trans. P. Hurd. Cambridge: Polity.

Lewis, I. M.

1986   *Religion in Context: Cults and Charisma.* Cambridge: Cambridge University Press.

Malamat, A.

1981   "Charismatic Führung im Buch der Richter." Pp. 110–33 in *Max Webers Studie über das antike Judentum: Interpretation und Kritik,* ed. W. Schluchter. Frankfurt am Main: Suhrkamp.

Neumann, P. H. A.

1979   *Das Propheten Verständnis in der Deutschsprachigen Forschung seit Heinrich Ewald.* Darmstadt: Wissenschaftliche Buchgesellschaft.

Rosenberg, J.

1986   *King and Kin: Political Allegory in the Hebrew Bible.*
Bloomington and Indianapolis: Indiana University
Press.

Schäfer-Lichtenberger, C.

1991   "The Pariah: Some Thoughts on the Genesis and
Presuppositions of Max Weber's *Ancient Judaism*," *JSOT*
51:85–113.

1995   *Josua und Salomo. Eine Studie zu Autorität und Legitimität
des Nachfolgers im Alten Testament.* Leiden: Brill.

Weber, M.

1952   *Ancient Judaism.* Trans. H. H. Gerth and D. Martindale.
New York: Free Press.

1963   *The Sociology of Religion.* Trans. E. Fischoff. Boston:
Beacon.

Whitelam, K. W.

1989   "Israelite Kingship: The Royal Ideology and its
Opponents." Pp. 119–40 in *The World of Ancient Israel*,
ed. R. E. Clements. Cambridge: Cambridge University
Press.

Wilson, R. R.

1980   *Prophecy and Society in Ancient Israel.* Philadelphia:
Fortress.

THE BOOK OF ISAIAH—A COMPLEX UNITY: SYNCHRONIC AND DIACHRONIC READING

Rolf Rendtorff

Today scholars are beginning to move from analysis to synthesis in the interpretation of the Book of Isaiah. The established practice of separating the book into several discrete parts, each of which is viewed in isolation from the whole, is giving way to exploratory efforts to understand the overall unity and the theological dynamic of the Isaiah tradition. Indeed, it is an illuminating experience to lay aside most of the commentaries of the past and read through in one sitting the Book of Isaiah with a kind of 'second naiveté' (Anderson: 17).

This quotation expresses some of the basic elements that built the starting point of the now seminar on "The Formation of the Book of Isaiah" in the framework of the Society of Biblical Literature, in which since a number of years scholars try to develop a new reading of this important book of the Hebrew Bible.[1] The intention of the present paper is first of all to review the various methodological approaches towards the reading of the book of Isaiah as a unity.

The question of the unity of the Book of Isaiah was reopened by Brevard Childs's canonical approach in *Introduction to the Old Testament as Scripture*, in which "Childs's most spectacular success is with the book of Isaiah" (Brueggemann: 89). Almost at the same time and independently of Child's work appeared Peter R. Ackroyd's article, "Isaiah I-XII: Presentation of a Prophet" (1978).

---

[1] This is a revised and updated version of my essay, "The Book of Isaiah: A Complex Unity. Synchronic and Diachronic Reading," in *New Visions of Isaiah* (ed. R. F. Melugin and M. A. Sweeney; Sheffield: Sheffield Academic Press, 1996 [forthcoming]).

This could be characterized as the other fundamental and influential contribution to this newly reopened debate. The comparison of these two works shows important basic agreements between the two scholars, in particular in the pronounced interest in the final form of the text; on the other hand, each of them approaches this question in a totally different way. In his powerful claim for the canonical unity of the Book of Isaiah, Childs concentrates on the book as a whole, and on the canonical interrelationships between its three commonly assumed historical parts. Ackroyd, for his part, throughout the entire book focuses on the question: "Why is there so substantial a book associated with the prophet Isaiah?" (1978: 21). He finds the "clue . . . in the actual structure of i-xii" (29), which he elaborates in detail.

Here emerged a number of methodological problems that have been much more diversified by the contributions of several other scholars. In addition, in retrospect it is visible that through the years time and again the question of the unity of the Book of Isaiah had been raised by individual scholars, some of whose observations and reflections now are taken up in the new broader framework.[2]

I

The common starting point among scholars interested in the formation of the Book of Isaiah and its unity is the conviction, or at least the assumption, that the present shape of the book is not the result of more or less accidental or arbitrary developments, but rather that of deliberate and intentional literary and theological work. As a rule, the question arises as how to define the leading methodological interest in exploring this work and its results. Childs speaks of "The Canonical Shape of the Book of Isaiah" (325). Other scholars, too, explicitly use the terms "canon," "canon-criticism," "canonical critical," and the like. All of them are

---

[2] I refer in particular to the works of Jones (1955), Liebreich (1955–56, 1956–57), Eaton (1959), Schreiner (1967), Becker (1968), Lack (1973), and Melugin (1976). For the history of research see also Vermeylen (1989: 11–27) and Williamson (1994).

aware of certain possible misunderstandings or misinterpretations. Ackroyd writes: "I do not for one moment fear that anyone will suppose that I am thereby disclosing myself as a biblical fundamentalist, though I may have to accept the dubious distinction of being misquoted as having abandoned one of the key points of critical scholarship" (1978:17). And he sums up:

> Canon-criticism, as a distinct area of discussion, involves a sensitive appraisal of both the final stages of the according of authority to the biblical writings, and the awareness of the different levels at which this has operated in the eventual determining of the texts which have come down to us, stamped with the hallmark of experiential testing in the life of the community to which they belonged (47–48).

It is indeed of particular importance to emphasize "the sensitive appraisal of both" (the final stages and the different levels) instead of playing off the awareness of the different levels against the keen interest in the final stage or stages. Childs writes: "To hear the different notes within the one book is an essential part of taking seriously the canonical shape" (330). And similarly other scholars using canon terminology are expressing their "indebtedness to historical analysis . . . which seeks to locate the text at prior historical moments" (Seitz, 1988:105).

R. E. Clements raises an objection against this canonical terminology: "Our problem is a literary and theological one of redaction criticism, not the larger and more problematic one of canon criticism, which we may set aside for discussion in the realm of hermeneutics" (1985:97). He argues that "the reasons why the book of Isaiah acquired its present shape" have nothing to do with the final "canonization" of the Hebrew Bible. He even declares that "it appears to be methodologically wrong to attempt to resolve these problems (i.e. of the Book of Isaiah) by an all-embracing hermeneutical appeal to the perspective of the canon" (n. 10).

The question raised has two different aspects. The first revolves around the understanding of the term "canon," while the second applies to the scholarly direction of research. In the framework of the current debate on the Book of Isaiah (as well as on other books of the Hebrew Bible), the term is mainly applied to the final shape of the respective book in which it eventually became part of the

canon as a whole. Therefore, it might be possible to discuss several
aspects of the formation of the Book of Isaiah without using the
term "canonical." Yet the more fundamental aspect of the question
has to do with the intention behind scholars' efforts to understand
the final form of a biblical book, in particular a book as important
as the Book of Isaiah, which is such a complicated one to be
understood as a whole. For a number of scholars, it is even the
"canonical" question that led them to this kind of exegetical work.
It would not make sense for them to set this question aside and
make such a strict distinction between exegesis and hermeneutics,
as Clements proposes. Therefore, the relevance and function of
the "canonical" aspect for the formation of the Book of Isaiah
needs to be discussed further.

II

The next set of questions concerns the three main parts of the
Book of Isaiah as they have been accepted by most scholars during
the last century. Even today the exploration of the formation of the
Book of Isaiah almost always starts from a point where the
existence of (Proto-) Isaiah (chaps. 1–39), Deutero-Isaiah (chaps.
40–55), and Trito-Isaiah (chaps. 56–66) is either taken for granted
or analytically discussed. This problem also has two major aspects.
One has to do with the prophetic figure behind each of the three
parts of the book; the other has to do with the literary unity and
independence of each part. The aspects are interrelated.

At this point the above mentioned methodological differences
between Childs and Ackroyd are particularly obvious. Childs does
not question the original existence of the three parts of the Book
of Isaiah (calling them First, Second, and Third Isaiah). With
regard to Second Isaiah, he assumes that there originally existed
certain elements showing the historical context of these
prophecies. Such elements later were eliminated, with the result
that these chapters lost "their original historical particularity."
Here Childs's canonical approach did not touch the classical
assumption of the earlier existence of several (at least two)
independent parts of the Book of Isaiah. Childs sees changes
happening only at the level where:

the canonical editors of this tradition employed the material in such a way as to eliminate almost entirely those concrete features and to subordinate the original message to a new role within the canon. (325)

Accordingly, he views the canonical editing of First Isaiah as a "coupling of collections," after which "a large amount of later material which is scattered throughout the entire collection. Moreover, both its older and newer elements have been structured into a clear theological pattern which is integrally connected with Second Isaiah" (330–31).

Ackroyd's approach is different. From the outset he questions the independent existence of chaps. 1–39 in particular as a collection of sayings of a prophet of the eighth century who was primarily a prophet of doom. In chaps. 1–12 he finds "a presentation of the prophet," "the messenger of doom, now fulfilled, as he is also presented as messenger of salvation" (1978:45). These chapters are composed of smaller units such as 1:2–2:5, 2:6–4:6, 5:1–11:16 (including 6:1–9:6), each of them containing oracles of doom and salvation. The psalm in chapter 12 "provides an interpretative comment on what precedes, drawing out in a final poetic statement the broadest significance of the prophet's person and message" (40). In his conclusion Ackroyd declares:

> It is not my intention to try to sort out either the genuine from the non-genuine, or the possible situations . . . to which this or that passage may belong, or in which re-application has been made (44). . . . Whether the prophet himself or his exegetes were responsible, the prophet appears to us as a man of judgment and salvation. (45)

The comparison of these two approaches shows a basic methodological problem with regard to the formation of the Book of Isaiah: Has the final form to be seen as the result of connecting or merging two (or three) originally independent parts (or books) by (one or more) redaction(s)—or is the originally independent existence of those parts no longer to be taken for granted? Among scholars working towards an understanding of the Book of Isaiah as a whole both positions are clearly represented.

With regard to the first position some qualifications are necessary. The question of Trito-Isaiah recently again has become subject of discussion (see below); therefore some scholars rather speak of relations between chaps. 1–39 and 40–66. With regard to the first part, some scholars set aside chaps. 36–39 as a later addendum, speaking of chaps. 1–35. But also chap. 35 is taken by some scholars as not having been part of the original collection of Proto-Isaiah, but being added as a redactional bridge between First and Second Isaiah. The common conviction of these scholars remains that a collection of First Isaiah sayings containing major parts of chaps. 1–39 had existed before having been combined with chaps. 40–66. For most of them this conviction includes a redactional reworking of certain parts of chaps. 1–39, be it in one or more redactional stages, even before their combination with chaps. 40–66. Widely accepted is the thesis of one (or two) redaction(s) in the time of Josiah and later after the fall of Jerusalem (Barth; Clements 1980b, 1980c). For Clements this is an important stage in the redactional history of the Book of Isaiah:

> Once the connection between the prophecies of Isaiah and the destruction of Jerusalem is recognized as a factor in the way the Book of Isaiah came to be developed, we have the single most essential clue towards understanding why the prophecies of chapters 40 and following came to be incorporated into the book. (Clements, 1982: 127)

Steck (1985) identifies chapter 35 as another crucial point for the connection between the two formerly independent collections. In a perceptive exegetical treatment he shows its interrelations in both directions—forward to chap. 40, and backward to chaps. 32–34. He concludes that chap. 35 had been formulated in order to be written in at the join between the end of the complex of sayings of First Isaiah (Isa 1–34), and at the beginning of Second Isaiah (Isa 40–62). He emphasizes that until then both parts had been independent of each other, and that each of them had been formulated in an unalterably fixed form (101).[3]

---

[3] Similarly, Clements (1982:121), who calls chap. 35 "a summarized 'digest' of the main content of the prophecies of chapters 40–55."

Both scholars represent characteristic examples of an approach to the Book of Isaiah that, on the one hand, strongly emphasizes the deliberate formation of the book as a whole while, on the other hand, firmly holds to the original independence of the first and the second part of the book from each other. From this point of view the final shape of the book is the result of a redactional process. The original parts are not touched by a "canonical" idea.

The most pronounced counter example is given by Seitz (1988). His provocative thesis is: "The whole notion of Second and Third Isaiah depends in no small part on there being a clear First Isaiah. Such an Isaiah is not to be found" (111). He emphasizes that "Isaiah 1–39 is an extremely complex collection of material, with a diverse background," and he claims that this has already been shown by several recent studies that "demand a complete rethinking of the relatively simple formulation 1, 2, 3 Isaiah" (n. 14). Indeed, the extremely complex character of chaps. 1–39 is conceded by almost all exegetes. The question is whether these divergent materials have been brought together before and independently of the joining of chaps. 1–39 with chaps. 40ff.

Steck, for example, declares explicitly that the main corpus of chaps. 1–39, before its connection with the following chapters, did exist in a fixed form whose formulation no longer could be touched (1985:101). According to his view, chap. 35 had been carefully worked in a way that it could build the bridge between the two now surrounding parts of the book. Some other texts—such as 11:11–16 and 27:(12)13 (as well as 62:10–12 in the second part)—share this bridging function with chapter 35. They express "the same redactional view."[4]

Clements also mentions texts in chaps. 1–39 that express the ideas of chaps. 40ff. Similarly to Steck he finds—in addition to chap. 35—in Isa 11:12–16; 19:32; 27:12–13: "summarizing assurances of the return of God's people to Zion . . . , which are

---

4 See the chart, Steck (1985: 80). The existence of an independent "Trito-Isaiah" is also denied by Vermeylen (1989:42ff), though his concept of the history of chaps. 40–55 is totally different from Steck's.

based upon the prophecies from chapter 40 on" (1982:121). Chapters 36–39, according to Clements, also have been added to chaps. 1–35 "at a time when much of the material of chap. 40 and following had already been joined to this earlier prophetic book" (123). Chapters 24–27 are "a very late section" which "should . . . not be regarded to be read in isolation of the rest of the book" (122). Those observations lead him to the suggestion "that the linking of the prophecies of chapters 40 and following with the tradition of Isaiah's prophecies belongs more fundamentally to the structure of the book" (123). That means that the junction of chaps. 1–39 and 40–66 appears not merely as one act of redaction at one certain point, but rather as a process by those elements of an earlier tradition ("Isaiah") that had been intertwined with those of exilic and postexilic traditions.

From this point of view, the difference between the positions of Clements and Seitz seemed to be reduced to the question whether there remains an identifiable "First Isaiah," which independently of the structure of the book as a whole has its own literary entity. Special emphasis should be given to Ackroyd's concept of a "presentation of a prophet," which questions the existence of definable "First Isaiah."

Another important point in Seitz's argumentation is that "the literary boundaries between 1, 2, 3 Isaiah are not marked in any special way" (109). Indeed, in Isaiah 40, no hint is given that now a new chapter begins, and that it is a different prophet who is speaking from now on; there is no evidence of a loss of any superscription or introduction. This problem is related to the question, which text had been read immediately before chap. 40 at the time when the two supposed collections had been combined. One argument for the clear definition of a new beginning in chap. 40 is the change of tone and content from doom to comfort. This seems to be true if chap. 40 was preceded by chaps. 36–39. But many scholars believe that these chapters had been inserted much later into the Book of Isaiah, probably as "one of the latest steps to occur in its formation" (Clements 1980:277), "thereby separating the different collections" (275). But if it is chap. 35 that has to be read before chap. 40, there is no change in tone and content. The

close relationship of chap. 35 to—or even dependent upon—
Deutero-Isaiah has been noted by many scholars. In Clements's
view, the argument turns the other way round: Not the difference,
but rather the similarity between the end of First Isaiah (now chap.
35) and the beginning of Second Isaiah (chap. 40) made the
connection possible or even more plausible.

Here again chaps. 36–39 have to be taken into account.
Ackroyd (1982) has convincingly shown a number of interrelations
between these chapters and chapters 1–12, in particular 6:1–9:6.
"Both these narrative or partly narrative sections . . . are evidently
concerned with themes of judgment and of deliverance" (19). And
these sections "alone in the book provide a full contextual setting
for the activity and message of Isaiah" (ibid.). Thus, not only chaps.
1–12, but also chaps. 36–39 could be called "presentation of a
prophet" (16). From chap. 39 it is obvious that God's words of
judgment against Israel will not become reality through the
Assyrians in the days of Hezekiah. The last words of the chapter
make it clear that it is only a sparing of Hezekiah and his
generation, and that the judgment will come in the days of the
Babylonians (also Melugin:177). Seitz summarizes his reading of
chaps. 36–39 as follows:

> A theological problem and a readership problem are solved in one
> fell swoop by the inclusion of chaps. 36–39. God's word of judgment
> over Israel's sins, declared in the Assyrian period by Isaiah, is to be
> fulfilled in the Babylonian period. At the same time, the reader is
> prepared for the words of comfort that appear in Isaiah 40ff, words
> that only make sense once the sentence of judgment, the 'time of
> service' of Isa. 40:2, has been carried out. (1988:111)

In the meantime, the connections between chaps. 36–39 and other
parts of the book have also been studied by Conrad (1988 and
1991), and more in detail by Seitz himself (1991).

III

The course of the discussion shows a changing approach to the
question of earlier collections of material now combined in the
Book of Isaiah. For some scholars the starting point still is the
more or less unquestioned existence of two or three "books" that

had been brought together by redactional work. With regard to chaps. 1–39, this includes a mainly diachronic reading of the texts led by the question about which stage of the redactional history a specific text had been formulated, reformulated, inserted, and the like. Other scholars are developing a different approach to reading chaps. 1–39 in their given form as parts of the book as a whole (Ackroyd; Seitz).

The later reading, with which I am sympathetic, does not mean a denial of diachronic questions but a change—and perhaps a reversal—of scholarly priorities. The first and main question is no longer what was the "original" meaning of this text? nor when and how had this text been incorporated into its present context. Rather, the question is: What is the meaning of the text in its given context? This does not exclude the first two questions to be asked for additional information and clarification. But the priority is now clearly given to the interpretation of the text in its given context.

This changing approach towards the Book of Isaiah has its first and most fundamental influence on the reading of chapters 1–39. "Isaiah 1–39 is an extremely complex collection of material," claims Seitz (1988, 111). Hence, if one reads chaps. 1–12 as deliberately composed "presentation of a prophet," then chaps. 1–12 will be understood as a meaningful composition in itself, comprising materials of different types and from different times, which depict Isaiah as a prophet of judgment and salvation (Ackroyd 1978:45). The diachronic question is not at all to be excluded, but can help to understand the interrelations between some of the texts that are now part of this composition.

A further application of this reading concerns the oracles against other nations of chaps. 13–23. Particularly important is the fact that this composition begins with an oracle against Babylon (chaps. 13–14). It shows that God's words of judgment spoken in times of the Assyrian rule will be realized by the Babylonians. Already at this point the borders from the times of First Isaiah to that of Second Isaiah are crossed (cf. Seitz 1988:112). From now on the reader is aware that the prophetic message of the Book of Isaiah is not restricted to the times of Assyrian rule, but embraces a time span going beyond that period into the Babylonian era. Then the transition from chap. 39 to chap. 40 does not come as a surprise to the reader. And even the further step from exile to return, i.e., from the Babylonian to the Persian era, has now been prepared.

Actually, this reading of the Book of Isaiah as embracing a long period of time with changing political events and experiences, begins, according to a certain view, in the first chapters of the book. It has been argued that chap. 1 forms a composition representing a summary of the prophetical message of "Isaiah" (Fohrer). Accordingly, this chapter contains elements that—at least on the part of later readers—can be understood as speaking from a point after the divine judgment had come over Israel. Verse 1:9 is taken by Clements "to be a late, exilic, addition in which the condition of Jerusalem after 587 was read back into Isaiah's prophecy of 701" (1980a:32). It is now a question of approach whether this reading back is taken as a late addition or as an integral element of the canonical presentation of the prophet. The same is true for the word on Jerusalem's fate in 1:21–28, in particular, its ending in verse 27f that "evidently supposes that Jerusalem had suffered severe setbacks" (35). Ackroyd summarizes his reading of 1:2–2:5, which ends with the eschatological role of Mount Zion:

> as an appeal and a promise: Jerusalem the unfaithful and judged city of God, over which the lament of 1:21ff is pronounced, is to be the true and faithful city, the center of the religious life of the world (1978:42).

This kind of observation and reflection leads to a new definition of "First Isaiah."

IV

The impact of the "totalic" approach to Isa 40–66 is different from its reading of chaps. 1–39. At first glance, there seems to be no influence of chaps. 1–39 on the later parts of the book. Yet already the beginning of "Second Isaiah" (40:1ff) poses questions that are unanswered without looking back to what precedes. The opening of chap. 40 without any introduction or superscription, and the call for comfort referring back to Jerusalem's "service" and her sins—these may allude the readers who know something of what had been said in the preceding part of the book.

In addition, the well-known parallels between Isa 40:1–8(11) and 6:1–11 have been recently re-examined by different scholars looking particularly for interdependencies between these two texts, which are pivotal in either part of the book (Melugin: 83f., Ackroyd 1982:5f., Rendtorff 1989:79ff., Albertz: 242ff., Seitz 1990). Albertz is mainly interested in the adoption and continuation of Isaianic motifs in Deutero-Isaiah, and he recalls the idea of an "Isaiah-school" as it had been raised earlier by Mowinckel and others. Other scholars reflect the possibility of a reciprocal influence on the level of composition or redaction (Rendtorff, Seitz). Accordingly, Childs emphasizes that the "former things" in Deutero-Isaiah in the context of the book as a whole "can now only refer to the prophecies of First Isaiah" (328ff; cf. Seitz 1988:110). But then the question arises as to what this expression might have pointed to at an earlier stage when chaps. 40–66 had not yet been combined with chaps. 1–39. Did the "former things" then mean anything different from earlier prophecies of judgment? And if not, which prophecies had they referred to? The question remains whether there could or should be assumed in chaps. 40–66 conscious references to chaps. 1–39. This question is also dealt with by Clements (1985), who mentions several topics by which he wants "to show that the evidence that the prophecies of "Second Isaiah" reveal a conscious dependence on earlier sayings of Isaiah of Jerusalem is firm and reliable" (1985:109).

Finally, in the course of looking at the Book of Isaiah as a whole the interrelations between "Second" and "Third Isaiah" are re-examined under different appearances. The most decisive step has been taken by Steck (1989) who, in the context of broad methodological reflections, denies the existence of a prophet or author "Trito-Isaiah." He sees chapters 56–66 as literary texts that never existed as a separate collection, but have stepwise been added to chapters 40–55 (so chaps. 60–62) or to a "Greater Isaiah" (*Großjesaja*), i.e., to the now emerging collection that included great parts of chaps. 1–39 and 40–55. This thesis is related to

Steck's earlier assumption (1985) that chap. 35 had been formulated in order to build the bridge between chaps. 1–39 and 40–55 at the time they were first combined.

Beuken's approach is different. He is also interested in Third Isaiah's relationship to First and Second Isaiah, which he describes as "Isaianic legacy" (1986). But he sees in Trito-Isaiah "a literary and theological personality in his own right" (1986:64), who is the successor of Deutero-Isaiah and, in a sense, also of Proto-Isaiah, and who "has used the prophecies of F(irst) I(saiah) and S(econd) I(saiah) for his particular message, in a situation that was quite different" (ibid.). Beuken's conviction of the unity and originality of Trito-Isaiah finds its specific expression in the development of "The Main-Theme of Trito-Isaiah," that of "the servants of God," which he finds as a "theme" through all chaps. 56–66, even where the expression itself does not appear (1990). A new debate is beginning, and we expect further work in this field. With regard to the Book of Isaiah as a whole of particular interest would be the question how developments in chaps. 40–66 are related to those within chaps. 1–39. For example, certain interrelations between chapters 1 and 66 have been observed by several scholars. Could it be possible that "those responsible for the last forming of the third part also contributed to the composition of the final shape of the book"? (Rendtorff 1984:319).

V

So far the present survey has not mentioned some contributions to the reading of the Book of Isaiah as a whole. In particular, one has in mind those that are not built up on questions of the structure of texts, but rather on certain themes, topics, expressions and so forth. My own first article in this area (1984) tried to show a number of topics and themes that are characteristic for the Book of Isaiah and at the same time appear in all—or at least in most of all—of the different parts of the book. My approach was influenced basically by Melugin and Ackroyd. My more recent article (1991) discusses the different meanings of the word צדקה in the context of the Book of Isaiah as a whole, including chaps. 56–66.

Another contribution that should be mentioned is that of Anderson. He faces the Book of Isaiah as a whole, but he writes that:

> Instead of reading the Isaiah tradition forward from the standpoint of the seminal preaching of Isaiah of Jerusalem . . . I propose to consider it from the viewpoint of its final apocalyptic *relecture* or rendering. (18)

That brings texts from all parts of the book in relation to each other in a new and often surprising way. Anderson keeps the diachronic aspects in mind; thus, his essay easily and fruitfully can be related to questions of the redactional or compositorial history of the texts. In general, I believe that this search for the totality of the Book of Isaiah should allow, and even requires, studies on topics, themes, expressions, and even ideas characteristic of the book as a whole, or considerable parts of it, without at the same time discussing the questions of redaction or composition.

VI

In sum, the discussion of the last decade has revealed a search for the unity of the Book of Isaiah. Of course, it is not a simple unity but a highly complex one. The methodological approaches regarding this issue of unity are different, as explained in detail in this paper. But it seemed to me to be nevertheless remarkable that in certain crucial points a basic agreement can be reached. One of the crucial points is the question of an independent book or collection of "First Isaiah," containing major parts of chaps. 1–39. The scholarly discussion shows that there is a broad agreement on the "secondary" character of elements like chaps. 13–23, 24–27, and, according to a number of scholars, also of smaller units like 2:1–5, 4:2–6, 12:1–6 and others. That makes it nearly impossible regarding this "secondary" reading to read the "original" parts (in whatever sense) of chaps. 1–39 as a continuous "book." Nevertheless, some scholars continue to speak of a "First Isaiah," thereby including some of the "secondary" elements. The commentary by J. H. Hayes and S. A. Irvine (1987) is one recent example of interpreting almost the whole of Isaiah 1–39 as deriving from the eighth-century BCE prophet. The authors explicitly mention the impact of Y. Gitay's work, "who has pioneered in the rhetorical analysis of prophetic speeches" (15). In the meantime appeared Gitay's book (1991), in which he presents his view with regard to chaps. 1–12. He also holds that Isaiah 1–12 in its entirety derives from the prophet Isaiah and is to be understood as a series of oratorical reflections. Therefore, the problem about how the complex unity of the Book of Isaiah came into being, as discussed in this paper, for him does not exist. Future research will have to show whether it would be possible to relate these different approaches to each other.

The position which reads the Book of Isaiah mainly in its given "canonical" shape, though in full awareness of its (diachronic) complexity provides, in my view, the great advantage of such a sophisticated synchronic reading—that the interpreter is able to read the text in its given continuity. To choose one example: Ackroyd (1978) reads chapters 1–12 as a complex unity, while according to Steck (1985:80) 4:2–6, 11:11–16, and 12:1–6 are added at different times, 12:1–6 having been inserted only "after 302/1." Then and earlier the entire present text according to this perspective will have been presented.

The main difference between these two approaches might be expressed by the following two questions: 1) (Synchronic) What does the text (in all its complexity) mean in its given final shape? 2) (Diachronic) In what stages did the text reach its final form? Certainly, these two questions are oversimplifying the complex character of the problems. Yet by this simplification I am intending, on the one hand, to point to a crucial difference between these two approaches; on the other hand, I seek to stimulate a discussion on the agreements and disagreements between these two positions.

Works Consulted

Ackroyd, P. R.
1978   "Isaiah I-XII: Presentation of a Prophet." Pp. 16–48 in
Congress Volume: Göttingen 1977. SVT 29; Leiden: Brill.
1987   "Isaiah 36–39: Structure and Function." Pp. 105–20 in
Studies in the Religious Tradition of Old Testament.
London: SCM.

Albertz, R.
1990   "Das Deuterojesaja-Buch als Fortschreibung der Jesaja
Prophetie." Pp. 241–56 in *Die Hebräische Bibel und ihre
zweifache Nachgeschichte* (Fs. R. Rendtorff). Neukirchen-
Vluyn: Neukirchener.

Anderson, B. W.
1988   "The Apocalyptic Rendering of the Isaiah Tradition."
Pp. 17–38 in *The Social World of Formative Christianity and
Judaism* (Fs. H. C. Kee), ed. J. Neusner. Philadelphia:
Fortress.

Barth, H.
1977   *Die Jesaja-Worte in der Josiazeit.* WMANT 48. Neukirchen-
Vluyn: Neukirchener.

Becker, J.
1968   *Isaias—Der Prophet und sein Buch.* SBS 30. Stuttgart:
Katholisches Bibelwerk.

Beuken, W. A. M.
1986   "Isa. 56:9–57:13—An Example of the Isaianic Legacy of
Trito-Isaiah." Pp. 48–64 in *Tradition and Reinterpretation
in Jewish and Early Christian Literature* (Fs. J. C. H.
Lebram). Leiden: Brill.
1989   "Servant and Herald of Good Tidings. Isaiah 61 as an
Interpretation of Isaiah 40–55." Pp. 411–42 in *The Book
of Isaiah—Le Livre d'Isaïe*, ed. J. Vermeylen. BETL 81.
Leuven: Peeters.

1990   "The Main Theme of Trito-Isaiah: The Servants of YHWH," *JSOT* 47:67–87.

Brueggemann, W.

1984   "Unity and Dynamic in the Isaiah Tradition." *JSOT* 29:89–107.

Carr, D.

1993   "Reaching for Unity in Isaiah." *JSOT* 57:61–80.

Childs, B. S.

1979   *Introduction to the Old Testament as Scripture.* Philadelphia: Fortress.

Clements, R. E.

1980a   *Isaiah 1–39.* Grand Rapids: Eerdmans; London: Marshall, Morgan and Scott.

1980b   *Isaiah and the Deliverance of Jerusalem.* JSOTSup 13. Sheffield: JSOT Press.

1980c   "The Prophecies of Isaiah and the Fall of Jerusalem in 587 B.C." *VT* 30:421–36.

1982   "The Unity of the Book of Isaiah." *Int* 36:117–29.

1985   "Beyond Tradition History: Deutero-Isaianic Development of First Isaiah's Themes." *JSOT* 31:95–113.

Conrad, E. W.

1988   "The Royal Narratives and the Structure of the Book of Isaiah." *JSOT* 41:67–81.

1991   *Reading Isaiah.* OBT 27. Minneapolis: Fortress.

Eaton, J. H.

1959   "The Origin of the Book of Isaiah." *VT* 9:138–57.

1982   "The Isaiah Tradition." Pp. 58–76 in *Israel's Prophetic Tradition* (Fs. P. Ackroyd). Cambridge: Cambridge University Press.

Fohrer, G.
1962   "Jesaja 1 als Zusammenfassung der Verkündigung Jesajas." *ZAW* 74:251–68. (*BZAW* 99:148–66).

Gitay, Y.
1991   *Isaiah and His Audience: The Structure and Meaning of Isaiah 1–12.* Assen: Van Gorcum.

Hayes, J. H. and S. A. Irvine
1987   *Isaiah. The Eight-Century Prophet: His Times and His Preaching.* Nashville: Abingdon.

Jones, D.
1955   "The Tradition of the Oracles of Isaiah of Jerusalem." *ZAW* 67:226–46.

Lack, R.
1973   *La symbolique de livre d'Isaïe.* AnBib 59. Rome: Biblical Institute Press.

Liebreich, L. J.
1955–56 "The Compilation of the Book of Isaiah." *JQR* 46:259–77.
1956–57 "The Compilation of the Book of Isaiah." *JQR* 47:114–38.

Melugin, R.
1976   *The Formation of Isaiah 40–55.* BZAW 141. Berlin & New York: de Gruyter.

Rendtorff, R.
1984   "Zur Komposition des Buches Jesaja." *VT* 34:295–320. (ET: *Canon and Theology,* Minneapolis: Fortress, 1993, pp. 146–69.)
1989   "Jesaja 6 im Rahmen der Komposition des Jesajabuches." Pp. 73–82 in *The Book of Isaiah—Le Livre d'Isaïe,* ed. J. Vermeylen. BETL 81. Leuven: Peeters. (*Canon and Theology,* pp. 170–80.)

1991   "Jesaja 56, 1 als Schlüssel für die Komposition des Buches Jesaja." Pp. 172–79 in *Kanon und Theologie. Vorarbeiten zu einer Theologie des Alten Testaments.* Neukirchen-Vluyn: Neukirchener. (*Canon and Theology,* pp. 181–89.)

Schreiner, J.

1967   "Das Buch jesajanischer Schule." *Wort und Botschaft: Eine theologische und kritische Einführhng in die Probleme des Alten Testaments.* Würzburg: Echter.

Seitz, C.

1988   "Isaiah 1–66: Making Sense of the Whole." Pp. 105–26 in *Reading and Preaching the Book of Isaiah,* ed. C. Seitz. Philadelphia: Fortress.

1990   "The Divine Council: Temporal Transition and New Prophecy in the Book of Isaiah." *JBL* 109:229–47.

1991   *Zion's Final Destiny: The Development of the Book of Isaiah: A Reassessment of Isaiah 36–39.* Minneapolis: Fortress.

Steck, O. H.

1985   *Bereitete Heimkehr: Jesaja 35 als redaktionelle Brücke zwischen dem Ersten und Zweiten Jesaja.* SBS 121. Stuttgart: Katholisches Bibelwerk.

1989   "Tritojesaja im Jesajabuch." Pp. 361–406 in *The Book of Isaiah—Le Livre d'Isaïe,* ed. J. Vermeylen. BETL 81. Leuven: Peeters.

1990   "Zions Tröstung. Beobachtungen und Fragen zu Jesaja 51, 1–11." Pp. 257–76 in *Die Hebräische Bibel und ihre zweifache Nachgeschichte.* (Fs. R. Rendtorff) Neukirchen-Vluyn: Neukirchener.

Sweeney, M. A.

1988   *Isaiah 1–4 and the Post Exilic Understanding of the Isaianic Tradition.* BZAW 171. Berlin & New York: de Gruyter.

Vermeylen, J.

1977–78 *Du prophéte Isaïe à l'apocalyptique,* 2 volumes. Ebib. Paris: Gabalda.

1989 "L'unité du livre d'Isaïe." Pp. 11–53 in *The Book of Isaiah—Le Livre d'Isaïe,* ed. J. Vermeylen. BETL 81. Leuven: Peeters.

Watts, J. D. W.

1985 *Isaiah 1–33.* WBC 24. Waco: Word.

1987 *Isaiah 34–66.* WBC 25. Waco: Word.

Williamson, H. G. M.

1994 *The Book Called Isaiah.* Oxford: Clarendon.

FREEING THE IMAGINATION: THE CONCLUSION TO THE BOOK OF JOEL

James L. Crenshaw

The last five verses in Joel give voice to fundamental human aspirations to live in security, to experience prosperity, to look on justice, and to attain permanence. The language by which these modest hopes achieve expression resonates with other utopian dreams scattered throughout the Hebrew Bible, leaving the impression of ideological affinity if not outright literary dependence. Still, the restraint in Joel 4:17–21 [English Versions, 3:17–21] contrasts markedly with the imagistic exuberance characterizing much of the book. In this essay I wish to examine this extraordinary conclusion to the prophetic book of Joel in the light of alternative descriptions of imagined bliss and to explore the relationship between 4:17–21 and 1:1–4:16.

4:17 And you will know that I Yahweh your God
　　　　reside in Zion,[1] my sacred mountain;
　　　　Jerusalem will be holy,
　　　　and strangers will not pass through it any more.

4:18 And on that day
　　　　mountains will drip sweet wine, hills will ooze milk,
　　　　and all water sources of Judah will overflow.
　　　　A stream will flow from Yahweh's house,
　　　　watering the valley of Shittim.[2]

---

[1] Alternatively, "And you will know that I am Yahweh, who resides in Zion . . . ."

[2] I understand the phrase to be symbolic, like the valley of Jehoshaphat, rather than a literal valley of acacias. It therefore becomes meaningless to search for its location, whether to the west of Bethlehem in the modern Wādi-es-Sánt or to the east of Jerusalem in the Wādi-ᶜen-Nār. My view also renders problematic Kapelrud's hypothesis about the importance of acacia wood in cultic use (170–71). Kapelrud, too, thinks the valley looks to the future. In this regard he concurs with Sellin (177), who writes that the valley (the name of

4:19 Egypt will be a desolation,
      Edom a wilderness waste,
      Because of violence against Judeans[3]
      When they spilled innocent blood in their land.[4]
4:20 But Judah will be inhabited for a long time,
      Jerusalem for many generations.
4:21 Truly I will consider their blood innocent
      that I have not considered innocent,[5]
      And Yahweh will reside in Zion.

The Concluding Section and the Rest of the Book

I have departed from something approaching scholarly
consensus by including verse 17 in the final unit (Wolff:74, 82–84;
Allen:122–26; Hubbard:81–84; Prinsloo:113–21; Kapelrud: 169;
Ahlström:134; Robinson and Horst:69, who argue for a chiastic
arrangement; Rudolph:1971). My reasons for doing so are far from
arbitrary. To begin with, virtually all interpreters recognize close
kinship between this verse (v. 17) and its sequel, which seems to
elaborate upon it. At the very least, verse 17 functions as a
threshold point, marking off the boundary between two distinct
sections but also serving as a means of entry from one to the
other.[6] For me, the inclusio[7] in 4:17 and 4:21, specifically "Yahweh

which he emends to demons, *haśśēdîm*) is concerned with a geography of the
end of the age.

[3] Context requires an objective accusative here; Judeans are victims of the
crimes, not the perpetrators.

[4] Syntax favors the land of Judah rather than Egypt and Edom. Accordingly,
Necho's murder of Josiah at Megiddo and Egyptian incursions by Sheshonq I
and Osorkon I qualify, as do the attacks against Jehoshaphat by a coalition of
Edomites, Ammonites, and Moabites. On the other hand, if "their land" refers
to foreign territory, one thinks of Jeremiah and his compatriots from Mizpah
who fled to Egypt and of the Jews at Elephantine, as well as Edom's harsh
treatment of Judeans fleeing from Babylonians in 587.

[5] The Septuagint and the Syriac read *nqm*, avenge, in 21aβ while the MT
reads *nqh*. I retain *nqh* in both instances of the verse, reading the first verb as a
prophetic perfect.

[6] "A threshold is in fact a point of contact and of separation, the symbol of
both an end and a beginning. It is static in that it marks a boundary; yet it is
dynamic in that it is meant for crossing" (Buccellati:35).

resides in Zion," offsets the illusion that the formula "On that day"[8] introduces a new unit. The statement of recognition in 2:27 and 4:17 ("And you will know that I am in the midst of Israel; truly I am Yahweh your God and there is no other" // "And you will know that I Yahweh your God reside in Zion, my holy mountain") serves as an inclusion for the entire book.[9] Hence my use of this stylistic device accords with ancient predilection either at the authorial level or at the redactional one.

Taking 4:17 as the beginning of a unit does not deprive the previous section of an appropriate ending. Ominous portents notwithstanding, Yahweh turns toward Israelites as a refuge and fortress while terrifying the nations with unnatural events and supernatuural manifestations of divine fury. If v. 17 really functions as a threshold, the reference to foreigners who will never again desecrate the sanctuary may designate the nations who are summoned to judgment in 4:9–16, as well as Egypt and Edom in 4:19.

This transitional role of 4:17 explains why so many scholars connect the verse to what precedes. Actually, the unity of the concluding verses is by no means self-evident, and their sequence appears strained (Bewer:143). Two things seem to disturb the harmony of the larger unit: the shift from first to third person address in 4:21 ("Truly I will consider . . . and Yahweh will reside . . ."); and the separation of 4:19b and 4:21a ("When they spilled innocent blood . . . Truly I will consider their blood innocent") by sentiment that otherwise provides a smooth ending to 4:19a ("Egypt will be . . . Edom . . . But Judah . . . Jerusalem"). The natural conclusion for 4:20 is, therefore, 4:21b ("And Yahweh will

---

7 Judicious use of the principle of inclusio often illuminates a text's structure, but excessive claims by some interpreters, e.g. Loader (1979) have rendered suspect any appeal to inclusio.

8 On "*bᵉyôm YHWH*," see especially Hoffmann (37–50) and Bourke (5–31, 199–212).

9 The formula combines features of recognition and self-introduction (Zimmerli:36–40). Against my interpretation, one could argue that the statement of recognition concludes the two parts of the book, with 4:18–21 functioning as a supplementary unit.

reside in Zion"). Lacking supporting textual evidence for such an original, and refusing to believe that redactors had so little grasp of stylistic subtlety, I choose to interpret the present text and to assume that its apparent flaws have some other explanation.[10]

I. *Sitting in the Rubble (1:1–2:11)*

I turn now to the task of understanding the concluding section of the book in terms of what goes before it. In 1:1–2:11 a description of past disaster, a locust plague, fades into a report of this attack in images of fire and an invading army. A devastating drought complicates matters further, threatening both humans and animals. A virtual garden of Eden is quickly transformed into a desert waste (2:3). A single impression rises above the vivid account of extreme want—the land is so dry that fire races across the stubble, leaving a blackened earth as if to mock the wilted twigs discarded by the locust horde and to indicate the hopelessness signified by water sources that have become dry. The contrast in 4:17–21 could hardly be sharper; Judah's mountains and hills drip a constant supply of liquid, water sources flow freely, and a river extends from the sanctuary to a valley beyond. This picture of abundant water, milk, and new wine exists alongside another that transfers the desolation from Judeans to bitter enemies, Egyptians and Edomites. A single phrase, "Zion my holy mountain," gives continuity to the earlier description of calamity and the later promise (2:1; 4:17).

Only the threat against Judeans specifies its audience, whereas the combined promise of weal for Judah and woe for its enemies offers a lone clue about the audience, the personal pronoun "you." Those addressed directly in 1:1–2:11 are to a large extent functions of the narrative: elderly citizens who alone can verify the unprecedented nature of the locust plague; drunkards, who feel most personally the burden of a failed grape harvest; farmers and vintners, who watch their labor come to naught; priests, who stand

---

[10] This tendency to concentrate on the final form of the text is one of the many contributions of literary interpretations of the Bible; I have discussed this approach in (1990:515–19) and have developed my own approach (1989:51–64).

before the sacred altar with empty hands because the ingredients for cereal and libation offerings have vanished. Together these groups comprise the audience of both sections, establishing the personal dimension lying behind the pronoun "you." On one occasion, the vocabulary becomes expansive, addressing "all inhabitants of the land" (1:12), but like the broad designation "Israelites" this reference restricts itself to Judeans.

The language of 1:1–2:1 betrays extraordinary interest in religious personnel associated with the cult and in priestly functions such as proclaiming fasts and sounding the alarm that summoned the populace for religious instruction. Three different designations exalt the priestly order as "ministers of the altar" (1:13), "ministers of Yahweh" (1:9–2:17), and "ministers of my God" (1:13). Likewise, three expressions occur for the act of celebration now missing from daily life: "joy" (1:12), "rejoicing" (1:16), and "exultation" (1:16). A joyless society suffers the misfortunes sent by its Lord. The divine promise in 4:17–21 does not elevate priestly personnel, although it assures the purity of Jerusalem and the permanent presence of deity.

What kind of community is reflected in these literary units? All signs point to a struggling agrarian society desperately trying to eke out subsistence against overwhelming odds. Locusts have devastated the grain and destroyed grape vines, figs, olive trees, fruit trees, dates and pomegranates. Even the cattle add their bewilderment to the grief felt by human owners. The text mentions no professional class beyond priests and agriculturalists,[11] but these are precisely the ones necessitated by the events themselves. Silence may therefore not reveal anything about the makeup of the threatened Judaen society, which may very well have had various crafts and professional guilds. Nevertheless, the implication that a locust plague brought virtual ruin can scarcely be denied, and that

---

[11] Note the diversity of professions enumerated in Sir 38:24–34. Ben Sira contrasts the scribe's privileges to the less desirable, but necessary, crafts: farmer, craftsman, smith, and potter. Even if Ben Sira draws on the Egyptian Instruction of Duauf, the text may accurately reflect Judean society, for the list of professions is much fuller in the Egyptian "Satire on the Trades."

acknowledgement leads to the conclusion that agriculture was the community's primary means of subsistence.

The further silence about other professional groups who would be endangered by the day of Yahweh, the second metaphor for the threat to the community, reinforces this conclusion. The text is ambiguous about whether or not that terrible day has actually arrived, juxtaposing a statement that the day has come with a qualifier, "It is near" (2:16). Unlike Israelites addressed by Amos, these Judeans harbored no illusions that this day would bring victory over their enemies. The ominous features of the day, which Amos emphasized in graphic detail (Amos 5:18–20), are intensified in Joel's description. Amos' account of that dark day depicts one-on-one danger. A person fleeing from a lion meets a bear, but escaping both, is bitten by a serpent in the deceptive safety of home. Joel, however, describes a mighty army of locusts whose coming obscures sun, moon, and stars, so that the only appropriate adjectives are *nôrā' me'od*, (exceedingly *awesome*)" and *mî yekîlennû* (*irresistible*) (2:11b). Just as fire devours dry stubble, this army marches relentlessly, scales the city wall, and enters windows like a thief. Here the text strings together three sources of terror: soldiers, fire, and thieves. The first is highly organized, the second random. and the third extraordinarily furtive. Like Amos, Joel envisions no escape from the devastation (2:3c). How, then, did the community secure the divine assurances nestled in 4:17–21?

II. Looking for a Way Out (2:12–27)

Deliverance from the ravages of Yahweh's punitive agents came through sincere repentance, expressed here in the metaphor of rending hearts rather than garments. The text introduces the remote possibility that Yahweh would relent even at this late stage ("Yet even now," 2:12). It does so in the strongest manner possible—through use of a solemn oracular formula, "whisper of Yahweh" (Vetter:2–3)[12]. This stylistic device accompanied by fasting, weeping, and remorse is possible because of Yahweh's

---

[12] The word *ne'ūm* occurs 365 times in the formula "whisper of" followed by a name for the deity. Only eleven occurrences are not connected in this way with divine speech.

character declared to Moses. Just like other canonical texts that appeal to the ancient confession in Ex 34:6–7 (Crenshaw, 1984:9), this one concentrates solely on Yahweh's positive attributes. Joel describes God as merciful, compassionate, long-suffering, abundantly loyal, and repentant of causing harm (2:13b). To be sure, Joel remembers divine freedom as well,[13] and this memory prompts him to shape the conclusion in the form of a rhetorical question functioning as a denial, "Who knows?" (Crenshaw, 1986:274–88). He may turn, repent, and leave a blessing—cereal offering and libation for Yahweh your God?" (2:14).

The text recounts in considerable detail the preparation for a ceremony of penitence involving everyone, even suckling infants and newlyweds. The prophet encourages the appropriate officials in language far from economical: blow the shofar in Zion, sanctify a fast, call a solemn assembly, and gather a congregation. Such lavish summoning of the populace functions to prevent any absentees from marring the event and frustrating its goal. As religious leaders of the gathered community, priests are instructed to enter the holy place and to implore Yahweh to have pity on one and all. The people of God thus seek to avoid the religious dilemma forced on them by disaster. In their misfortune they offer conclusive evidence in the eyes of foreigners that Yahweh has either abandoned them or does not really exist (Buber:199–210). Nehemiah, the governor of Judah under Persian hegemony, individualizes this plea, using the rare verb ḥūsāh (pity) also and relying on Yahweh's abundant loyalty, kerōb ḥasdekā (Neh 13:22).

The desire to escape mockery at the expense of foreign frivolity has left its mark on several biblical texts. Psalm 79 complains that foreigners ask, "Where is their God?" (v. 10) and that the taunters have defiled the sanctuary by spilling blood like water (79:1,3). The result of such cruelty is that foreigners reproach the victims (cf. Joel 2:17). The same question is embedded in Ps. 42:4,11 (E.V., 42:3,10), but the mocker may this instance actually be a member of

---

[13] Not every liturgy of repentance achieved its desired result, for divine freedom sometimes asserted itself because of the burden borne by the deity. An example is Jer 14:1–15:9 (Crenshaw 1984:50–56).

the Israelite community. Elihu's use of this question is both hypothetical ("None asks, 'Where is God my maker who gives songs in the night?'" Job 35:10) and antithetical (that is, it emphasizes Yahweh's kindness rather than absence). Psalm 115 associates the question with foreigners but also stresses Yahweh's loyalty and faithfulness (vv. 1–2). This mocking question appears in prophetic literature (Mic 7:10 and Mal 2:17), although issuing from the lips of a personal enemy in the former case, and denying divine justice in the latter.

The decisive turning point of the book takes place at 2:18, which declares that Yahweh had compassion on land and people. The rest of chapter two announces the reversal of Judah's misfortune, and promises an abundance of the foodstuffs devoured by locusts. In addition to satisfying physical hunger, Yahweh recognizes the psychological impact of mockery, vowing never again to submit the people to such reproach. Indeed, the Lord goes one step further, promising to drive out the northerners, a term that seems to conjure up every kind of fear lurking in the psyche of Judeans.[14] Likewise, Yahweh determines to quench thirst and to banish desolation beyond the eastern or western seas.

Using an ancient expression for allaying anxiety in God's presence (Stähli:765–78), Joel urges land and animals not to fear and proposes joyous exultation in its place. In the wake of a return of herbage and fruit, Judeans happily celebrate Yahweh's name. Point for point the deity promises a complete reversal of everything that the locusts destroyed. The ancient recognition formula concludes Yahweh's promise, but this expression of certainty is flanked front and back by a solemn declaration that these humiliated Judeans will never again be subjected to shame (2:26b–27).[15] Armed with divine promises, the Judean community can once more confidently face the future.

---

[14] The enemy from the north in the book of Jeremiah evokes this same fear, one brought on by constant armies spilling over the land of Judah (and Israel) from Syria, most having originated elsewhere in Assyria and Babylonia.

[15] Consult Stolz:1979. The term occurs frequently in prophetic texts, but also 34 times in Psalms.

III. Dreaming of Another Day (3:1–4:16)

Egalitarian interests occasionally erupted in Israelite society where religious functionaries enjoyed special privilege. Priestly groups, obliged to defend their fee structure,[16] argued that as a tribal entity they had given up all claim to territorial inheritance when the land was allocated to the several family units. In their view, this voluntary renunciation of an inheritance entitled priests to demand special payment from the populace for services rendered. Cultic prophets also enjoyed a lifestyle made possible partly by the fees they levied and partly by royal patronage.[17] Their possession of the spirit, or more accurately, the spirit's possession of them, more than once seems to have occasioned flights of fantasy. An example of wishful thinking survives in the story about Eldad and Medad, who prophesied in the Israelite camp and encountered Joshua's opposition until Moses defended their zeal with the following words: "Are you jealous on my behalf? I wish all Yahweh's people were prophets and that the Lord would put his spirit in all of them" (Num 11:29).

The prophetic designation, "man of the spirit," indicates the importance of possession by the spirit, and at least one prophet felt constrained to boast about the full measure of divine spirit empowering his message (Mic 3:8). Other prophets stressed the visionary dimension of their vocation, one that resulted in two technical terms, *rōʾeh* and *ḥōzeh* (seer). Still other prophetic figures emphasized the word, which they interpreted as divine authorization; this dimension of prophecy gave rise to the common designation *nābîʾ* (the called one). It appears that the representatives of these three different ways of viewing prophecy

---

[16] In contrast to Josh 14:3–4, which omits the tribe of Levi in allocating the land, Ezek 48:8–14 envisions a substantial territory being given to the priestly groups, Zadokites and Levites, in the midst of which stands the Temple.

[17] The story about Saul's search for lost asses throws light on ancient attitudes about consulting seers. According to 1 Sam 9:5–10, Saul recognized the need for some sort of gift when approaching a seer for counsel. Interestingly, a servant had a small piece of silver although Saul had brought along nothing of value.

competed for recognition by the populace,[18] although at least one historiographer, the Deuteronomist, insists on continuity between diviner and *nābîʾ* (1 Sam 9:9). Each mode of intermediation enountered difficulty of one sort or another. The *spirit* generated excessive behavior and could not always be trusted, according to the story about Micaiah ben Imlah's confrontation with court prophets loyal to King Ahab (1 Kgs 22). *Visionaries* suffered from a bad press in the episode featuring Balaam, and subsequent endorsement of visions by Amos failed to dissuade others like Jeremiah who felt threatened by prophets with opposing views arising from what he took to be bogus dreams and visions. The *word* also posed a problem, for its enigmatic quality necessitated interpretation and, according to Num 12:6–8, only Moses received unambiguous messages from Yahweh. All other prophets encountered the divine word as obscure riddles, and the resulting rival interpretations did little to encourage the people, who relied on prophets for spiritual guidance, to put their trust in anyone (Crenshaw, 1971).

Moses' spoken wish that all God's people were prophets lingered in the minds of pious Judeans until the prophet Joel once more gave it currency. He cautiously locates such a wondrous phenomenon in the future;[19] the only time frame he provides is the adverb "afterwards." In the context of the book this temporal designation harks back to the divine promise that disaster will be replaced by its opposite. Like Moses' wish, Joel's articulation of

---

[18] Sigmund Mowinckel's hypothesis (199–227) that early Israel's emphasis on the spirit suffered an eclipse during eighth century classical prophecy but enjoyed resurgency during the sixth century with Ezekiel, Haggai, and Zechariah offers a plausible explanation for curious gaps in some prophetic literature with respect to the spirit as a means of authorization.

[19] In this respect Luke's use of Joel's prophecy in describing the remarkable infusion of the spirit during Pentecost cannot be faulted (Acts 2:1–21). Luke's citing of Joel 3:1–5a has some interesting features: the addition of an oracular formula to identify the divine speaker; the location of the event "in the last days"; the inversion of references to young men and old men (does this shift correspond to a shift in attitude from honoring maturity of years to revering youthful athletes?); the possessive pronoun attached to the servants (they are God's property!); and the omission of 3:5b, the promise of survivors on Mt. Zion and beyond.

divine intent is limited to Judeans, despite the appearance of universalism in the expression "all flesh." The restrictive nature of the outpouring of the spirit gives way in one significant regard, for slaves, both male and female, will experience the power of god's spirit in the same way as do free Judeans. The rushing spirit manifests itself differently in its recipients, bringing harmony where opposition once reigned. Children will proclaim the divine word; their elders will dream; and young people will have visions. Such a religious community will not confront the perennial problem of testing intermediaries (Wilson, 1980), for in this ideal situation everyone has direct access to the divine will.

Pneumatic theology was deficient in one respect, for it did not convince outsiders, in Joel's case, foreigners. Hence from the speaker's point of view (Berlin:43–82; Sternberg:129–52; Bar-Efrat:13–45; Alter, 1981; Bal, 1985), the addition of astrological phenomena seems intended for external consumption. Yahweh threatens to inaugurate signs and portents—blood, fire, and ominous cloud—in the sky and on earth. These forebodings of apocalyptic thought stop short of pondering about a fiery holocaust.[20] Instead, they focus on a solar eclipse and a blood-red moon as harbingers of a far more dreadful event, the dawn of Yahweh's day. Two adjectives, *haggādôl* (great) and *weḥannôrā'* (awesome), suffice to release pent-up emotions associated with suppressed anxiety.

In contrast to other biblical texts in which emphasis falls on the total absence of any escape, this one takes a different form. Invocation of Yahweh's name opens an avenue of escape, particularly if it takes place in the holy city. Joel bases such assurance on divine promises from the past. What about Jews who had the misfortune of residing outside Zion? Does any hope exist for them? The reference to survivors, which gives the impression of an afterthought,[21] may allude to captives of earlier wars who have

---

[20] Scholarly understanding of apocalyptic has changed remarkably in recent years. My own views have profited greatly from reading Collins (1984), Smith (131–56).

[21] BHS proposes to transpose "and in Jerusalem" from 3:5b to 3:c, thus arriving at the translation, "And in Jerusalem survivors whom Yahweh calls."

managed to endure the hardships associated with transported subjects. In their case, Yahweh does the calling.

The bold thought of survivors beyond the Judean hills triggers additional wanderings of the imagination. After all, cosmic portents imply universal rule on Yahweh's part, and this significant reality should translate into rescue for people who call upon the deity. The tables will be turned on Judah's conquerors, for judgment on the nations has been delayed too long.

This day of judgment will be located in the valley of Jehoshaphat, probably an imaginary place.[22] Chosen for its symbolic value, the name affirms that Yahweh will judge. These guilty nations have offended both Yahweh's inheritance, Israel, and the land apportioned to them. Joel specifies the particular crimes for which the nations must pay: casting lots over the people of God, selling a boy for the price of a harlot and a girl for the cost of wine *which they drank*. The final verb in Hebrew, *wayyištû* (and they drank it) registers the prophet's utter contempt for the conduct of these victorious soldiers.[23] For this act of greed Tyre, Sidon, and Philistines will be judged. Not content with valuables of this kind, they entered into a thriving slave trade, selling Judeans to Greeks, who relocated them in a faraway place. For their cruelty these sea-loving peoples will watch their own children being sold by the Judeans to Sabeans, who live in the desert.[24] This punishment is an appropriate one, for Judeans, who had no love for the sea, had been sold to sea-faring people.

---

[22] "The 'valley-plain of Jehoshaphat,' just like 'the northerner' in 2:20 and the 'valley of the acacias' in 4:18b, is a cipher; the use of such was quite popular in the emerging apocalypticism" (Wolff:76); ". . . hence a theological symbol rather than a topological one" (Prinsloo:105); "this valley cannot be located on any map; it, too, belongs to the sphere of mythology" (Kapelrud:147).

[23] The word *lᵉhêkᵉlêkem* (4:5) may also refer to palaces; in all likelihood, some of the booty was confiscated by high ranking soldiers for their personal use— even if placing the valuable vessels in foreign sanctuaries heaped indignity on a defeated deity.

[24] Wolff (77–78) writes that slave trade between Greece and a coalition of coastal peoples including Tyre, Sidon, and Philistines flourished from the fifth century until 343 BCE, but he adds that during the fourth century Phoenicia was subject to strong Greek influences.

The positioning of the two oracular formulas in the book of Joel suggests that the prophet recognized the fantastic dimension within such announcements. Once more Joel introduces divine authority for his own description of final retribution against the enemies at whose hands Judeans suffered humiliation and physical abuse. "For Yahweh has spoken"—this simple statement prevents Joel's audience from dismissing everything as idle speculation or wishful thinking. Now the hearers must reckon with a claim that the promises are grounded in Yahweh's integrity.[25]

Martial imagery bristles in what follows. Whereas Judeans were instructed to sanctify a fast, the nations are commanded to do likewise to a battle. Reversing ancient tradition about an era of peace, Joel urges the nations to beat their plowshares into swords and their pruning hooks into spears. Even their weaklings are told to boast of military valor. The description of Yahweh entering into judgment in the valley of Jehoshaphat betrays its origins within an agrarian community. The sickle will fell the harvest and the treader will extract juice from grapes. The language itself signifies the gravity of the offense, repetition of the word $h^{ae}m\hat{o}n\hat{i}m$ (4:14) heightens the emotional intensity in the face of utter confusion in the valley of decision. The dreaded day of Yahweh has drawn near at last. In addition to the astrological portents here repeated, the day witnesses Yahweh's self-manifestation and an accompanying earthquake. Joel uses the same language that opens the book of Amos: "Yahweh roars from Zion and utters his voice from Jerusalem" (Joel 4:16a; Amos 1:2a).[26] Safely hidden in Yahweh, a refuge and fortress, God's people, Judeans and Israelites, escape the judgment finally directed against the nations.

---

[25] Readers of sacred texts often forget that truth claims are not self-validating. Even the formula of recognition, which might carry an element of legal proof, hardly persuades anyone who is not already committed to belief. The reverse-side of proof from stupendous events is equally cogent; failure of the deity to act decisively can be read as weakness, at the least, and non-existence at the extreme.

[26] Whereas Amos localizes the repercussions of the divine appearance, Joel universalizes its effects. I have discussed Amos' use of theophanic language; see Crenshaw (1968:203–15).

Utopian Visions Outside the Book of Joel

Thus far I have examined the relationship between 4:17–21 and what precedes this concluding section. I wish now to consider the dominant ideas within comparable descriptions of a better day. I shall concentrate on the following biblical texts: Amos 9:11–15; Mic 4:1–4; Isa 2:2–4; 11:6–9; Ezek 47:1–12; Zech 14:1–21; Mal 3:19–21 [E.V. 4:1–3] and Gen 49:10–12.

At least three macro-themes stand out in these texts:

1. nature's transformation;
2. the restoration of the greatness of the Davidic dynasty;
3. the inauguration of an era of peace.

The absence of any allusion in Joel 4:17–21 to the Davidic dynasty may result from the position of the priests in the Judean community which the prophet addressed. If one assumes a date for the book in the fifth or fourth centuries,[27] recent precedent from the period of Haggai and Zechariah would provide an object lesson against an active messianism (see Meyers and Meyers:336–75). The tightly governed Ptolemaic era did not countenance political unrest in the name of restoring Davidic rule. If Joel actually draws on Amos 9:11–15 and Gen 49:10–12, the book does so selectively. From the latter may come the mention of milk in the depiction of fertility, although this idea may derive from the ancient tradition about Canaan as a land of milk and honey; and from Amos 9:11–15 comes the reference to the bountiful flow of sweet wine from the mountains. Both Amos and Ezekiel surpass Joel 4:17–21 in the scope of fertility, with overlapping sowing and

---

[27] I do not place much confidence in our ability to determine dates for ancient texts, although I believe it essential to attempt to do so. A few facts seem to indicate a date after the building of the temple in 521–516 BCE under the leadership of Haggai and Zechariah: silence about a king over Judah; the reference to an active temple cult; the mention of a city wall; the allusion to slave trade between Greeks and Phoenicians; the reference to Sabeans in this context as well; the character of the language; the stage of proto-apocalyptic thought in the book; the use of earlier canonical literature, especially Obadiah, Zephaniah, Ezekiel and Zechariah 14; and the absence of any reference to Assyrians and Babylonians. On the other hand, Rudolph (1967:193–98) argues strongly for the late pre-exilic period, Myers (177–95) prefers 521–516 BCE.

reaping, on the one hand, and prolific plants that mature in a month, on the other hand. Curiously, the picture of fertility in Hos 14:5–7 [4–7] does not appear to have influenced Joel 4:17–21.

Joel's reference to the nations' journey to Judean territory has nothing comparable to the pilgrimage for religious instruction in Mic 4:1–4 and Isa 2:2–4. Nevertheless, Joel uses the concept of Yahweh's judgment of the nations, which ushers in an era of peace. At the same time, he reverses the wonderful sentiment about beating swords into plowshares and spears into pruning hooks, applying the new version to a doomed army. The notion of healing in Ezek 47:1–12 and Mal 4:1–3 does not appear in Joel's account, whereas the life-giving stream does. This river that flows from the sanctuary in Jerusalem plays an important role in Ezek 47:1–12 and Zech 14:1–21, in the latter of which streams flow to the east and to the west. It follows that the closest affinities exist between Joel 4:17–21 and Ezek 47:1–12 and Zech 14:1–21. These three themes and virtual silence with respect to the exquisite imagery in Hos 14:5–7; Isa 11:6–9, 9:1–7; and Mic 4:1–4//Isa 2:2–4 must surely indicate priestly preferences of the author responsible for Joel 4:17–21.

Perhaps the most striking feature of Joel's description of a better day is its restraint. If one is going to dream, why not dream big? It remains a mystery why this unusual text modestly envisions nothing more than Yahweh's presence to assure a holy place, an ample supply of wine, milk, and water, revenge on enemies for the spilling of innocent blood, and a permanent title to the Judean hills. Other dreamers certainly set their sights higher, if one can judge from their robust language. The beauty of Joel 4:17–21 lies in its response to the suffering occasioned by calamity and the resultant soul-searching. Small wonder the inclusio in this unit focuses on Yahweh's residence in Zion. This author believed that Yahweh's abode in Jerusalem guarantees security for those who take refuge there. In a very real sense, this inclusio corresponds to the ecstatic shout with which Ezekiel concludes: "*Yahweh šammāh*," ("Yahweh is there!"). Where Yahweh resides, one need not fear locust plagues, drought, fire, or armies. That message in Joel 4:17–

21 provides an effective conclusion to a book in which ominous threats play such a prominent role.

Works Consulted

Ahlström, G. W.

    1971   *Joel and the Temple Cult of Jerusalem.* VTS 21. Leiden: Brill.

Allen, Leslie C.

    1976   *The Books of Joel, Obadiah, Jonah and Micah.* Grand Rapids: Eerdmans.

Alter, R.

    1981   *The Art of Biblical Narrative.* New York: Basic Books.

Bal, M.

    1985   *Narratology.* Toronto: University of Toronto.

Bar-Efrat, S.

    1989   *Narrative Art in the Bible.* Sheffield: Almond.

Berlin, A.

    1983   *Poetics and Interpretation of Biblical Narrative.* Sheffield: Almond.

Bewer, J. A.

    1911   *A Critical and Exegetical Commentary on Obadiah and Joel.* ICC. Edinburgh: T. & T. Clark.

Bourke, J.

    1959   "Le jour de Yahvé dans Joël." *RB* 66:5–31, 191–212.

Buber, M.

    1968   *On the Bible.* New York: Schocken.

Buccellati, G.

    1981   "Wisdom and Not: The Case of Mesopotamia." *JAOS* 101:35–47.

Collins, J. J.
    1984   *The Apocalyptic Imagination.* New York: Crossroads.

Crenshaw, J. L.
    1968   "Amos and the Theophanic Tradition." *ZAW* 80:203–15.

    1971   *Prophetic Conflict.* BZAW 124. Berlin and New York: de Gruyter.

    1984   *A Whirlpool of Torment.* Philadelphia: Fortress.

    1986   "The expression of *mî yôdaʿ* in the Hebrew Bible." *VT* 36:274–88.

    1989   "Clanging Symbols." Pp. 515–19 in *Mercer Dictionary of the Bible,* ed. Watson E. Mills. Macon: Mercer University.

    1990   "Literature, Bible as." Pp. 515–19 in *Mercer Dictionary of the Bible,* ed. Watson E. Mills. Macon: Mercer University.

Hoffmann, Y.
    1981   "The Day of the Lord as a Concept and a Term in The Prophetic Literature." *ZAW* 93:37–50.

Hubbard, D. A.
    1989   *Joel and Amos.* Downers Grove: Inter-Varsity.

Kapelrud, A. S.
    1948   *Joel Studies.* Uppsala: Lundequistska.

Loader, J. A.
    1979   *Polar Structures in the Book of Qohelet.* BZAW 152. Berlin and New York: de Gruyter.

Meyers, C. L., and E. M. Meyers
    1987   *Haggai, Zechariah.* AB 25B. Garden City: Doubleday.

Mowinckel, S.
    1934   "The 'Spirit' and the 'Word' in the Pre-exilic Reforming Prophets." *JBL* 53:199–227.

Myers, J. M.
1962   "Some Considerations Bearing on the Date of Joel."
        ZAW 74:177–95.

Prinsloo, W. S.
1985   *The Theology of the Book of Joel.* BZAW 163. Berlin and
        New York: de Gruyter.

Robinson, T. and F. Horst
1954   *Die Zwölf Kleinen Propheten.* HAT 14. Tübingen: Mohr.

Rudolph, W.
1967   "Wann wirkte Joel?" *BZAW* 105:193–98
1971   *Joel, Amos, Obadiah, Jonah.* KAT 13,2. Gütersloh: Mohn.

Sellin, E.
1929   *Das Zwölfprophetenbuch.* KAT 12. Leipzig: Deichertsche.

Smith, J. Z.
1975   "Wisdom and Apocalyptic." Pp. 131–56 in *Religious
        Syncretism in Antiquity*, ed. Birger Pearson. Missoula:
        Scholars Press.

Stähli, H. P.
1979   *"yr'* fürchten." Pp. 765–78 in *Theologisches Handwörter-
        buch zum Alten Testament I*, ed. E. Jenni and C. Wester-
        mann. München: Kaiser.

Sternberg, M.
1985   *The Poetics of Biblical Narrative.* Bloomington: Indiana
        University.

Stolz, F.
1979   "*bôš* zuschanden werden." Pp. 269–72 in *Theologisches
        Handwörterbuch zum Alten Testament, I*, ed. E. Jenni and
        C. Westermann. München: Kaiser.

VanderKam, J. C.
1984   *Enoch and the Growth of an Apocalyptic Tradition.* CBQMS
        16. Washington D.C.: The Catholic Biblical Association.

Vetter, D.

1979   "*ne'um* Ausspruch." Pp. 2–3 in *Theologisches Hand-wörterbuch zum Alten Testament, II*, ed. E. Jenni and C. Westermann. München: Kaiser.

Wilson, R.

1980   *Prophecy and Society in Ancient Israel.* Philadelphia: Fortress.

Wolff, H. W.

1977   *Joel and Amos.* Hermeneia. Philadelphia: Fortress.

Zimmerli, W.

1979   *Ezekiel.* Hermeneia. Philadelphia: Fortress.

PROPHET AND PROPHECY:
AN ARTISTIC DILEMMA

Zefira Gitay

Prophetic literature is visually expressed through various artistic media. The art works focus either on the figure of the prophet, or on the prophetic utterance. The artistic depiction of the prophetic *word* either seeks to reflect upon the subject matter in general or on a specific prophetic verse. Therefore the artistic dilemma is whether to produce the prophetic representation as a reflection of the message as a whole, or of a particular verse, or to portray the prophetic figure as a symbol of the whole. In both cases the artist has to render visually either a personal impression (the personality of the prophet) or the prophetic word. This sort of artistic translation contributes to our understanding of prophetic literature. This interpretative dimension of the visual arts is a neglected field in prophetic hermeneutics, a gap which the present paper seeks to deal with.

Already in the Dura-Europus synagogue (3rd century CE) the walls were decorated with numerous illustrations of biblical scenes, among them "the vision of the prophet Ezekiel about *the Dried Bones*" (Ezek 37). The artist who portrays the revival of the bones does indeed show the valley of the scattered bones, but he included as well the sequence of the prophecy and its fulfillment through the miraculous transformation of the bones into living people (vv. 9–10). The biblical account is rich in imagery that easily enables the artist to translate vividly the written word into visual imagery, that is, the animation of the *Dried Bones*: ". . . O dry bones, hear the word of the Lord" (v. 4); the arrival of the four winds: ". . . say to the breath, Thus says the Lord: Come from the four winds, O breath, and breathe upon these slain . . ." (v. 9), or the march of the great army: ". . . and the breath came into them, and they lived, and stood upon their feet, an exceedingly great host" (v. 10).

The strong contrast between *the Dried Bones*—". . . The hand of the Lord was upon me . . . and set me down in the midst of the valley, it was full of bones" (v. 1), and the process of their revitalization by the blowing wind, filling them with the human spirit: "Thus says the Lord God to these bones: Behold, I will cause breath to enter you, and you shall live" (v. 5)—is powerfully portrayed by the artist. The scenes follow the order of the prophecy step by step: from the valley and the scattered bones to the bodies lying like dead figures while the spirit, the *psyche*, awaits to enter into the lifeless corpses. Finally, the portrayal shows the people standing ready to march forward as an army (v. 10) (*Fig 1*). Moreover, the composition not only dwells on the prophecy and the process of transforming the bones into human beings, it also sustains the prophet who is portrayed in the scene, not once, but six times. The artist is therefore not satisfied with the portrayal of the visual imagery of the prophecy alone; he chooses to strengthen it through the appearance of the prophet himself in the act of delivering the message. The visual imagery is therefore a precise and detailed account of the prophetic discourse, depicting the Word of God as follows: (1) "The hand of the Lord was upon me, . . ." (v. 1); (2) and then: "he said to me: Prophesy to these bones . . ." (v. 4); (3) as the story continues, the prophet says: "I prophesied as I was commanded . . ." (v. 7); (4) ". . . he said to me: Prophesy to the breath . . ." (v. 9); (5) "I prophesied as he had commanded me . . ." (v. 10); (6) "Thefore, prophesy, and say to them . . . I shall put my Spirit within you . . ." (vv. 12–14).

The analysis of the illustration of the prophetic message suggests that the artist consulted the written text, following it to the detail. However, the fact that the artist repeatedly adds Ezekiel's figure to his illustration is a complex problem because the prophet's portrayal is not confined to his appearance in the scene only as a representational figure. The prophet is portrayed six times when he is directed in his acts by the hand of God, which is not only a visual representation of God's word; it has its root in the text of verse 1: "The hand of the Lord was upon me . . .". Yet if this had been the depicted subject, then the six figures of the prophet would all be alike. We are, however, confronted with the artist's decision to represent Ezekiel in two different costumes. The first is the Parthian costume which appears four times, while the other, the Roman costume, appears twice. Is this only because the artist wishes to create a more complex composition, or is this because the prophecy combines two aspects, "death" and "life," which necessitates the portrayal of two figures of the prophet. The preference is to portray the prophet as a Parthian leader while prophesying to the *Dried bones*. However, in the two scenes in which the *Dried bones* are being transformed into human beings, and "spirit" takes over as a result of the blowing wind, the artist uses a figure in a Roman attire.[1] The text's imagery enables the artist to transfer the *word* into his medium in a creative manner. It appears that for the artist the inclusion of the prophet is essential, even though the focus is on the prophecy itself. The artist of Dura-Europus seems to search for a balance between the representation of the prophetic message and its messenger. He is aware of the relationship between the two and seeks to bridge them, even if the prophetic text does not supply any information about the physical appearance of the prophet. However, a question is raised: is the image of Ezekiel intended to portray the prophet himself, or does it allude to a powerful contemporary leader that, in the case of the prophecy of the *Dried bones*, is transformed into the figure of Ezekiel?

The costumes of the represented figures suggest that the artist transposes the image of the prophet Ezekiel into his own period and place which is the Roman provincial town of Dura-Europus on the border with Persia (Goldman:74). According to the artist's contemporary milieu the image of a local leader of the community serves as a prototype for the prophet's portrait. The role of the artists who illustrate historical moments is therefore also to provide their viewers with an understandable composition that is a mirror

---

1 Goldman (64) points out that Ezekiel as a Jewish spiritual leader had worn the non-Jewish royal costume, however he was also portrayed in a robe such as other great Jewish personalities like Moses wore.

that is to be accessible and appealing to the viewer's experience. It is already the British artist, Sir Joshua Reynolds (1732–1792), who points out in his *Discourse on Art* that:

> A painter of portraits retains the individual likeness: a painter of history shows the man by showing his actions . . . He has but one sentence to utter, but one moment to exhibit. He cannot, like the poet or historian, expatiate, and impress the mind with great veneration for the character of the hero or saint he represents, though he lets us know at the same time, that the saint was deformed, or the hero lame . . . He [the painter] cannot make his hero talk like a great man; he must make him look like one. (Reynolds: 58)

The historical portrayal is not only an archaeological depiction but also a reflection of the artist's present environment.

On reading the prophetic utterance, it generally appears that the artists have no difficulties in choosing the subjects for their portrayal, and yet, there are very few references to the prophets' characteristic features. Therefore, if the artists seek to express the act of delivering the message (as did the artist of Dura-Europus), they need to create a representational image of the prophet. This is a constant dilemma for the artist because there is a need to fill in missing details. In any event, because the prophecies are designed to be fulfilled in the future, the artist finds that the contemporary costumes and styles are not out of order.

An example is the case of the "peaceful days to come" of Isaiah (11:1–10). The American Quaker artist Edward Hicks (1780–1849), since 1823 repeatedly portrayed his *Peaceable Kingdom*. Hicks not only visually translated the written words of the prophet into imagery, but he wrote them as well, creating the frame for the picture (Fig 2).[2]

> The wolf also shall dwell with the lamb, and the leopard shall lie down with the kid; the calf and the lion and the fatling together; and a little child shall lead them. (Isa 11:6)

---

[2] Hicks resorted many times to writing as a frame to his *Peaceable Kingdom* (1823–25); later on he added the sentence: "When the great Penn his famous treaty made with Indian chiefs beneath the elm tree's shade" (1826, 1828–30). (Ford: 46–55; 59–76.)

The artist depicts the animals and the young child who leads them as they appear in the verse, that is, on the right side. They are arranged in a pastoral landscape, enjoying each other's company. On the other side, the left, the river flows slowly, almost embracing the stones under the bridge. However, Hicks does not dwell on the prophetic message of Isaiah alone; a group of Indians and Americans are greeting each other in the background. For the artist, the elements of the landscape in this composition are both an artistic medium as well as a message. The message offers a vision that transforms the *Peaceable Kingdom* from the prophet's era to current events in America. The artist adds a detail in regard to the legendary Treaty scene of Penn and the Indians which took place on the banks of the Delaware river. As a result, Hick's Isaiah's prophecy is symbolic, representing his own message as well. Notice that the artist does not change the prophetic message. On the contrary, he follows the prophetic words to the letter, but as he illuminates the prophecy he takes the freedom to transform it into his contemporary viewers' own experience.

The artist, however, does not confine his portrayal to the prophecy alone (as Hicks does), but also depicts the prophet himself (Dura-Europus). The point is that the prophetic books allude to the prophet's feelings. Hence the artists are stimulated to express those feelings as well. The case of Jonah is illuminating, because the focus of the artist is not only on the prophecy itself but on the story of the prophet who is running away from the injunction to prophecy as well. As a result, his unsuccessful escape ends with an unusual event: he is swallowed by the fish (2:1). Later on, the fish vomits Jonah on to the shore (2:11), where he is protected by the castor-oil plant (4:6). This miraculous event has opened the door for rich creative artistic depictions because it is not a reality that the artist must portray but a surrealistic subject: a man who is swallowed by a fish and returns alive. The Renaissance artist, Michelangelo, creates the portrayal of *Jonah* (Fig 3) on the ceiling of the Sistine Chapel. The prophet is portrayed above the altar with a branch above his head and the fish leaning over his leg (De Tolnay: 52, 150–51). The artist portrays Jonah with the two artifacts that connect the figure of the prophet with his activities.

The portrayal creates a disquieting figure that is marked by his surroundings, and he turns his head upward seeking help while his hand points downward to the source of his emotional upheaval. The image of a tremendous Jonah who appears to be bending backwards (Vasari: 130) evokes wonder and amazement in the viewer. The artist's focus is on the prophet, but the prophecy is integral to the composition; both are inseparable. However, the prophecy is secondary to the power of the prophet's image for the viewer. Jonah has to be distinguished from other prophets in order to portray his uniqueness. Thus, the artists rely upon symbols in order to identify the individual prophet for their viewers.

However, it is Michelangelo's creative power which enables him to portray Jonah's image without even relying on the features of the book, as E. Male had noted:

> It must, however be confessed that it needed the power of a Michelangelo to draw an adequately impressive portrait of them [the prophets]. (Male: 159)

In the case of the book of Jonah, the text is sufficiently rich. The portrayal of the prophet is therefore able to remind the viewer of his adventures and their consequences, as noted by the art historian, M. Schapiro:

> The text is often so much fuller than the illustration that the latter seems a mere token, like a pictorial title; one or two figures and some attribute or accessory object, seen together, will evoke for the instructed viewer the whole chain of actions linked in that text with the few pictured elements. . . . (Schapiro: 9)

As the role of the prophet in his prophecy is dictated by the nature of the prophetic discourse, it seems that artists who wish to dwell on the prophet's personality have to refer to the prophetic message in their visual portrayal. This does not mean, however, that the portrayal of the prophet is conditioned by the prophecy, but that characteristic features will create an immediate association between the prophets' image and their identity. For instance, when Rembrandt creates the image of *The Prophet Jeremiah* (Fig 4, 1630) he depicts the prophet at the most crucial moment in his life: the fulfillment of his prophecy about the destruction of Jerusalem (Jer

32:2–5). It is not only the prophecy that is being fulfilled, but the prophet himself is a living witness to the forceful outcome of his message to the people:

> Nebuchadnezar king of Babylon gave command concerning Jeremiah through Nebuzaradan, the captain of the guard, saying, 'Take him, look after him well but deal with him as he tells you' (39:11–12).

He sees the destruction of his city (39:8) and the exile of its people to Babylon (39:9). This is a tragic event, and the prophet is therefore portrayed by the artist when he is lamenting over the fall of city of Jerusalem: ". . . to fulfill the word of the Lord by the mouth of Jeremiah, until the land had made up for its Sabbaths. All the days that it lay desolate . . ." (2 Chron 36:21; cf Hoekstra: 150). Rembrandt is not as interested in the destruction of Jerusalem as a documentation of the prophecy as he is in exploring the feelings of the grieving prophet. The background is a reminder of the burning city, and the prophet mourns its fate. Rembrandt portrays Jeremiah leaning on the book, closing his eyes as if to avoid the disastrous reality that overwhelms him.

Is it the content of the prophecy that affects the artist or is it the need to portray the intriguing person behind the prophecy? The illustrations discussed above show that the richness of prophetic discourse has been a natural source of inspiration for artistic composition. However, the artists still do not restrict their composition to the prophecy alone. Time and again the prophet appears in conjunction with his prophecy, and many times the prophet's portrayal overwhelms his prophetic discourse. Nonetheless, the lack of details regarding the characterization of the person behind the prophecy creates a problem: how does one visually portray a prophet that the viewer is able to identify or relate to.

It is not enough to allude to the symbol of the prophet alone; the artist has to resort to the written word as well in order to overcome the anonymity of the prophet. For instance, artists insert the words of the prophet on a scroll in order to indicate who the illustrated prophet is. It might not always be necessary to resort to the written word; it might even be redundant, but the artist who wants to focus on the prophet rather than on his prophecy takes all precautions to enable the individual behind the message to be identified.

In the image of the *Prophet Isaiah*, (Fig 5) at Chartres Cathedral (The North Transept 13th century), the prophet is carved in stone carrying an open scroll on which the vision of Isaiah about the *Tree of Jesse* was originally written (Favier: 94). In his other hand there is a rod which bursts into flower at the top of the image towards which the prophet is pointing (Kidson: 200). However, in spite of the importance of the prophecy of Isaiah (11:1–10), the artist of Chartres has focused on the image of the prophet himself, only alluding to the prophecy by using the symbol of the rod and the written text of the prophetic message.

The image of the prophet Isaiah could then be identified either by the inscription or by its location in the layout of the Cathedral near to the statue of the Virgin. The location of the image is linked to the content of the prophet's prophecy: "There shall come forth a shoot from the stump of Jesse, and a branch shall grow out of his roots" (Isa 11:1; Male:162). However, it is possible that the artist does not really intend to dwell on the prophet but rather on the prophecy, using the prophet for the sake of his message. In Chartres itself there is a stained glass window which illustrates in detail the *Tree of Jesse*, a popular subject during the thirteenth century (Male:166). Thus, it is quite unlikely that the Chartres depiction of the prophet seeks to deal with the prophecy. It is the prophet who occupies the central stage in the layout of the cathedral, and the artist wishes to portray him.

In instances when the artist chooses to portray the prophet, there is a danger that the illustration will turn out to be imaginative and unrealistic. When there are no portraits of the prophets, and when the text itself is not rich with detailed literary description of the individual prophets, the artists have no choice but to invent their own prototype. Theoretically, because the image only needs to represent the person, any figurative illustration could serve the purpose. In this situation, however, the viewer may not be able to identify the individualized personality.

The American artist John Singer Sargent (1856–1925) creates *The Frieze of the Prophets* at The Boston Public library (1890–1919; Fig. 6). Sargent, a prominent portrait painter, is invited to create a mural which he calls *The Triumph of Religion*, in which the prophets are part of the design. Jeremiah, Isaiah, and Habakkuk are depicted as individuals whose emotions differ from one another. They have no symbolic objects that could identify them; it is only the titles that identify each prophet.

Sargent is known to create slightly unorthodox simplified compositions of his models, so it is not surprising that he was fascinated by the prophets' portrayal. He elegantly creates his images with remarkable expressions, but he does not use symbols of statues (Fisher: 92). Thus, it must have been a challenging goal for an artist, such as Sargent, whose goal is to effect realism, to recreate images from the past that leaves no detailed information. He recreates the biblical prophets as imaginary figures, but at the same time as a portraitist the artist is realistic, and does not romanticize the theme (Griffith: 90).

In 1890 Sargent finds that this task is enormous and he decides to explore the authentic people of the biblical land. He writes thus:

> The consequence of going up the Nile is, as might have been foreseen, that I must do an Old Testament thing for the Boston Library . . . . (Olson: 169)

Later on, when Sargent prepares the sketches for the mural, he asks his models, mostly Mediterranean Italians, to pose for him, bearing the weight of heavy blankets and posing with their arms up in a prophetic posture (Olson: 183). As a result, *The Frieze of the Prophets* mural comes nearest to achieving his life-long ambition to be as good a mural decorator as portrait painter. The most famous image of the entire mural of *The Triumph of Religions* is that of the prophets who as individuals appeal to their audience. They struggle to be heard, and their emotions create not only a schematized representation, but a human illustration of individuals. Olson suggested that these portraits of the prophets are:

... simple, direct and honored the purpose of the commission. It was
not a breathless performance but, rather, a heroic rendition of what
Sargent could see; he was back on familiar territory. (182)

However, despite the fact that Sargent has succeeded in creating
personalized portraits, they are nameless. He needs to resort to the
word in order to overcome the anonymity of the prophets without
their symbols. Like his predecessors, he exploits artistic ingenuity
in order to explore the human factor of the prophetic message,
the prophets themselves.

In conclusion, it is almost impossible for the artist to deal with
an abstract concept without inserting the speakers and their image.
Hence, the question is whether the artist's interpretation of visual
imagery is valid for understanding and supporting the literary
analysis of the text. As the artists are confronted with the problematic issues of translating the word into images, they have to resort
to an interpretative mode. It is therefore quite important for the
critic to identify and examine the major issues that the artist may
have to deal with when faced with the dilemma of portraying the
prophet, or his prophecy. At the same time, we must question what
might be the expectations of the viewer from the artistic creation.

The artists who are invited by their patrons to create figurative
expressions for biblical prophecies are creating a decorative
abstract composition. They use their skill to compose images and
forms in order to tell a story. Their artistic illustration has to be
clear enough for the audience, who must be able to identify the
subject that is depicted by the artist. If, however, there is a plan,
and visual imagery is not created only as a decorative element, then
this imagery must be planned according to a thematic religious
programmatic outline. This would mean that most of the artists are
not limited in their biblical compositions to the decorative
elements of artistic expression, and they must rely on their own
interpretation as well as on an interpretation of the text that
conforms to the religious views of the patron or to their own
religious views. It is interesting that artists who might be inspired
by the rich prophetic discourse have sought to explore the
struggles and the emotions of the individual, the prophet. They
focus on the person behind the *word*, the prophet. Thus the

prophet and his prophecy become interlocked. For the artist, the prophecy is illuminated by the prophet, and the understanding of the prophetic message depends upon the individual prophet. The artist who reads the text through his/her visual medium might, therefore, offer a fresh perspective on the prophets and their prophecies.

Works Consulted

Favier, J.
  1990   *The World of Chartres*, London: Thames and Hudson.

Fisher, L. E.
  1985   *Masterpieces of American Paintings.* Greenwich, CT: Brompton.

Ford, A.
  1985   *Edward Hicks: His Life and Art.* New York: Abbeville Press.

Goldman, B.
  1973   "Dura Costumes and Parthian Art." Pp. 53–77 in *The Dura-Europus Synagogue*, ed. J. Gutman. Missoula, MT: American Academy of Religion/Society of Biblical Literature.

Goodenough, E. R.
  1964   *Jewish Symbols in the Greco-Roman Period, Symbolism in the Dura Synagogue,* vol 10. New York: Pantheon.

Griffith, W., ed.
  1925   *Great Painters and Their Famous Bible Pictures.* New York: W. H. Wise.

Hoekstra, H.
  1990   *Rembrandt and the Bible.* Utrecht: Magna.

Katzenellenbogen, A.
  1959   *The Sculptural Programs of Charters Cathedral.* New York: Norton.

Kidson, P.

  1969   "The Transept Program." Pp. 194–206 in *Chartres Cathedral*, ed. R. Branner. New York: Norton.

Male, E.

  1954   *The Gothic Image.* London and Glasgow: Collins.

Olson, S.

  1986   *John Singer Sargent His Portrait.* London: Barrie & Jenkins.

Reynolds, J.

  1961   *Discourses on Art.* New York: Collier Books.

Schapiro, M.

  1973   *Words and Pictures.* The Hague and Paris: Mouton.

Sukenik, E. L.

  1947   *The Synagogue of Dura-Europus and its paintings.* Jerusalem: Bialik. (Hebrew.)

Tolnay De, Ch.

  1945   *The Sistine Ceiling.* Princeton: Princeton University Press.

Vasari, G.

  1927   *The Lives of the Painters, Sculptors, and Architects*, vol 4. London: Dent; New York: Dutton.

Illustrations

Figure 1. Dura Europus Synagogue, *The Vision of the Dried Bones by the Prophet Ezekiel.* Photo courtesy of the Yale University Art Gallery.

Figure 2. Edward Hicks, *Peacable Kingdom.* Photo courtesy of the Yale University Art Gallery.

Figure 3. Michelangelo, *The Prophet Jonah*. Photo courtesy of Art Resource.

Figure 4. Rembrandt, *The Prophet Jeremiah*. Photo courtesy of the Rijksmuseum.

Figure 5. Chartres Cathedral, *The Prophet Isaiah*. Chartres, France.

Figure 6. John Singer Sargent, *The Prophets Jeremiah, Jonah, Isaiah, Habakkuk*. Photo courtesy of Boston Public Library.

SUGGESTIONS FOR FURTHER READING

Andinach, P. R.

1992   "The Locusts in the Message of Joel." *VT* 42:433–41.

Bergler, S.

1988   *Joel als Schriftinterpret.* Frankfurt am Main: P. Lang.

Carreira, J. N.

1991   "Charisma und Institution. Zur Verfassung des Königtums in Israel und Juda." Pp. 39–51 in *Prophetie und geschichtliche Wirklichkeit im alten Israel* (Festschrift S. Herrmann), ed. R. Liwak and S. Wagner. Stuttgart: Kohlhammer.

Carroll, R. P.

1989   "Prophecy and Society." Pp. 203–26 in *The World of Ancient Israel,* ed. R. E. Clements. Cambridge: Cambridge University Press.

1990   "Whose Prophet? Whose History? Whose Social Reality? Troubling the Interpretative Community Again: Notes towards a Response to T. W. Overholt's Critique." *JSOT* 48:33–49.

Crenshaw, J. L.

1994   "Who Knows What Yahweh Will Do? The Character of God in the Book of Joel." Pp. 197–209 in *Fortunate the Eyes That See. Essays in Honor of David Noel Freedman,* ed. A. H. Bartlett et al. Grand Rapids: Eerdmans.

1995   *Joel.* AB 24C. New York: Doubleday.

Deist, F. E.

1988   "Parallels and Reinterpretation in the Book of Joel: A Theology of the Yom Yahweh." Pp. 63–79 in *Text and Context: Old Testament and Semitic Studies for F. C.*

Fensham, ed. W. Claassen. JSOTSup 48. Sheffield: JSOT Press.

Flanagan, J. W.

1988   *David's Social Drama.* JSOTSup 73. Sheffield: Almond.

Gitay, Y.

1995   "The Individual versus the Institution: The Prophet versus His Book." Pp. 279–92 in *Religion and Reconstruction of Civil Society,* ed. J. W. de Gruche and S. Matrin. Pretoria: University of South Africa.

Hiebert, T.

1992   "Joel, Book of." *ABD* 3:873–80. New York: Doubleday.

Hurowitz, V. A.

1993   "Joel's Locust Plague in Light of Sargon II's Hymn to Nanaya." *JBL* 112:597–603.

Jeppesen, K.

1988   "The Day of Yahweh in Mowinckel's Conception Reviewed." *JSOT* 2:42–55.

Kaiser, O., et al., eds.

1986   *Texte aus der Umwelt des Alten Testaments II/I. Religiöse Texte. Deutungen der Zukunft in Briefen, Orakeln und Omina.* Gütersloh: Mohn.

Laato, A.

1996   *History and Ideology in the Old Testament Prophetic Literature.* CBOTS 41. Stockholm: Almqvist and Wiksell.

Launderville, D.

1989   "Joel: Prophet and Visionary." *TBT* 27:81–86.

Loretz, O.

1986   *Regenritual und Yahwetag im Joelbuch.* UBL 4. Altenberge: CIS.

Mariottini, F. D.

1987   "Joel 3:10 (H 4:10), 'Beat Your Plowshares into Swords.'" *Pers* 14:125–30.

Mayes, A. D. H.

1989   *The Old Testament in Sociological Perspective*. London: Marshall Pickering.

1993   "Prophecy and Society in Israel." Pp. 25–42 in *Of Prophets Visions and the Wisdom of Sages. Essays in Honor of R. Norman Whybray*, ed. H. A. McKay and D. J. A Clines, JSOTSup 162. Sheffield: Sheffield University.

Nash, K. S.

1989   "The Cycle of Seasons in Joel." *TBT* 27:74–80.

Noort, E.

1977   *Untersuchungen zum Gottesbescheid in Mari*. AOAT 202. Neukirchen-Vluyn: Neukirchener; Kevelaer: Butzon & Bercker.

Ogden, G. S.

1987   *Joel and Malachi: A Promise of Hope. A Call to Obedience*. ITC. Edinburgh: Handsel; Grand Rapids: Eerdmans.

Overholt, T. W.

1990   "Prophecy in History: The Social Reality of Intermediation." *JSOT* 48:3–29.

Petersen, D. L.

1984   *Haggai and Zechariah 1–8. A Commentary*. OTL. London: SCM.

Prinsloo, W. D.

1992   "The Unity of the Book of Joel." *ZAW* 104:74–80.

Redditt, P. L.

1986   "The Book of Joel and Peripheral Prophecy." *CBQ* 48:225–40.

Romerowski, S.

 1993 "Joel et le Culte," *BRT* 3:18–35.

Saags, H. W. F.

 1978 *The Encounter with the Divine in Mesopotamia and Israel.* London: Athlone.

Seitz, C. R.

 1996 "How is the Prophet Isaiah Present in the Latter Half of the Book? The Logic of Chapters 40–66 within the Book of Isaiah." *JBL* 115:219–40.

Simkims, R.

 1991 *Yehweh's Activity in History and Nature in the Book of Joel.* ANETS 10. Lewiston, NY: Mellen.

Toorn K. van der

 1987 "From Patriarchs to Prophets. A Reappraisal of Charismatic Leadership in Ancient Israel." *JNSL* 13:191–218.

INDEX OF AUTHORS

INDEX OF SUBJECTS